INTELLIGENCE AND CONTEMPORARY CONFLICT

Communication in Diplomacy, Statecraft and War

INTELLIGENCE AND CONTEMPORARY CONFLICT

Communication in Diplomacy, Statecraft and War

EDITED BY

MATTHEW HEFLER

BOKFÖRLAGET STOLPE

CONTENTS

INTRODUCTION

Matthew Hefler

'Secret intelligence is 'the missing dimension of diplomatic history'.'

This was the judgement of British diplomat Sir Alexander Cadogan. During the Second World War, Cadogan served as the Permanent Under-Secretary at the Foreign Office. This made him and his staff the key link between the Foreign Secretary and Britain's intelligence services. Few have had better knowledge of the critical role played by intelligence and secret services in war, diplomacy and statecraft.[1]

Ever since Cadogan's words were employed by Christopher Andrew and David Dilks in their pioneering study published in 1984, they have appeared in countless works of intelligence history. Yet their significance has not been diminished by repetition. Indeed, Cadogan's observation stands as a reminder of the perennial importance of secret intelligence and clandestine activities to both peace and conflict.[2]

This lesson was driven home on a global scale by Russia's invasion of Ukraine in 2022. As the conflict approached, allied intelligence services stepped to the fore in dramatic fashion, wielding declassifications of secret material to check Russian intentions, virtually in real time.[3] The ongoing war has continued to highlight the centrality of intelligence and communication to all aspects of contemporary conflict, from public diplomacy to intelligence-sharing to the maintenance of allied coalitions.

More recently, the world was shocked by the sudden and brutal invasion of Israel by Hamas militants. The attack – coming almost exactly 50 years after the Yom Kippur War, when Israel was surprised by invasions on two fronts – caught Israeli defence and security forces completely off guard. Claims of a colossal 'intelligence failure' spread quickly in the wake of the assault, drawing comparisons to 9/11 and Pearl Harbor.[4]

Never before has the role of intelligence and secret services so dominated the global agenda. To explore these issues, the Axel and Margaret

Ax:son Johnson Foundation and Bokförlaget Stolpe presents this collection of essays. *Intelligence and Contemporary Conflict: Communication in Diplomacy, Statecraft and War* brings together some of the world's leading intelligence scholars and practitioners to address key questions of intelligence and international security. In 12 concise essays, these experts draw on the insights of history to examine the connection between secrecy and communication in modern statecraft and conflict.

Intelligence and Contemporary Conflict was motivated in part by the war in Ukraine, and the themes around intelligence and secret services underscored by that conflict. Most notable of these was the role of allied intelligence services in the realm of 'public diplomacy' in the lead-up to the invasion – in particular the release of previously classified material, largely by American and British services, in an effort to articulate the reality of the Russian threat and to counter hostile efforts and disinformation in the information space.[5]

Yet if the Ukraine war highlighted issues around intelligence, it did not invent them. 'Intelligence as information is as old as government; so too is secret intelligence,' wrote the late Michael Herman, former secretary of the United Kingdom's Joint Intelligence Committee (JIC) and one of the world's leading intelligence 'practitioner-academics'.[6] *Intelligence and Contemporary Conflict* is divided into four sections, each with a series of essays exploring the role of secret and open information in starting or stopping conflict and in waging war from the past to the present.

The first section is entitled 'Intelligence and Communication from the Past to the Present'. Gill Bennett gets the ball rolling, exploring the key forms the communication of intelligence can take. This allows the former chief historian of the British Foreign and Commonwealth Office to illuminate the paradoxical aspects of secrecy itself. Next, Michael Goodman, official historian of the JIC, addresses a critical issue in an age of rising conflict: instances of intelligence as a warning of attack. My own contribution examines intelligence relationships between foreign intelligence services, such as that between the United States and the UK. It uses declassified material to shed light on the way clandestine relations can contribute to wider international diplomacy.

The second section is entitled 'Intelligence and Contemporary Conflict' and focuses on four of the world's most pressing strategic or diplomatic challenges. John Ferris, authorised historian of the Government Communications Headquarters (GCHQ), the UK's signals intelligence agency, examines intelligence and the war in Afghanistan. He applies a sweeping historical gaze to connect strategy, perception and hubris across multiple attempts to pacify the country, and in the process examines NATO's failed counterinsurgency. Next, Calder Walton of the Harvard Kennedy School turns to the invasion of Ukraine to explore the use of intelligence in public diplomacy. Using an applied history methodology, his contribution examines the record of US declassifications, from the Cuban Missile Crisis to the Iraq War. Sara Bush Castro looks at a critical instance of nuclear proliferation: that of China. By examining problematic assumptions that coloured CIA assessments of China's nuclear ambitions, she highlights errors of judgement that all analysts should seek to avoid. Finally, Steven Wagner confronts the ongoing conflict between Israel and Hamas. His contribution offers a critical early look into the intelligence failures revealed by the 7 October attack against Israel, and presents insights into how intelligence – and its failure – must be understood.

The third section is called 'Information, Assessment and Accountability', and turns to contemporary issues of intelligence in the information space. Suzanne Raine brings her deep institutional knowledge to an examination of the UK's Review of Intelligence on Weapons of Mass Destruction, also known as the Butler Review, 20 years after its release. Philip Davies of Brunel University London delivers a critical analysis of a high-profile example of intelligence as communications product: the UK Defence Intelligence department's daily updates on the war in Ukraine. This sophisticated assessment goes beyond the update to examine the strengths and weaknesses around the use of 'conditional language' in UK analytic 'tradecraft'. Daniela Richterova of King's College London provides a timely exploration of Russia's information and influence campaigns in the Global South in the context of the Ukraine war. Her contribution explores the continuity – and key differences – in Moscow's military, security and intelligence engagement in Africa, from the Cold War to today.

The final section, 'Communication and Contemporary Conflict', takes readers up to the cutting edge of technology and military tactics. Tony Ingesson of Lund University examines communications and secrecy in warfare. By analysing the way technology both enables and constrains military action, he illuminates the relationship between technology and tactics on the battlefield. To conclude, Matthew Ford of the Swedish

Defence University explores the transformative role of the smartphone in contemporary conflict. Perhaps most notably, he argues that this technology will go beyond shaping military tactics to changing the very nature of the combatant.

There is little doubt that the world is entering a more dangerous and uncertain period. Increased competition and a multitude of transnational challenges place a growing strain on established international structures and norms. As insecurity and instances of conflict grow, national and international security mechanisms must rise to the occasion. It is more important than ever to understand the work of the national intelligence services that contribute to the decision-making of statecraft.

This collection represents a timely contribution to important debates around contemporary conflict. It bears on a range of pressing issues through contributions from some of the finest intelligence scholars and practitioners in the world, who seek to address current issues by harnessing the insights of history and practical expertise. We hope these essays can inform, inspire and advance the discourse on many facets of contemporary conflict and international security.

Stockholm, Sweden, June 2024
Matthew Hefler

1. See John Ferris, *Behind the Enigma: the Authorised History of GCHQ, Britain's Secret Cyber-Intelligence Agency*. London: Bloomsbury, 2020, p. 272; David Dilks (ed.), *The Diaries of Sir Alexander Cadogan, OM, 1938–1945*. New York: G P Putnam's Sons, 1971; Keith Jeffery, *MI6: the History of the Secret Intelligence Service, 1909–1949*. London: Bloomsbury, 2010, p. 597; Richard J Aldrich, *GCHQ: the Uncensored Story of Britain's Most Secret Intelligence Agency*. London: Harper Press, 2010, pp. 44–70. His role in practice: see The National Archives (TNA), FO/1093/235; Christopher Andrew and David Dilks (eds.), *The Missing Dimension: Governments and the Intelligence Communities in the Twentieth Century*. London: Palgrave Macmillan, 1984.

2. See Ferris, *Behind the Enigma*; Christopher Andrew, *The Secret World: a History of Intelligence*. London: Penguin, 2019.

3. Brett M Holmgren, Assistant Secretary, Bureau of Intelligence and Research, US Department of State. Intelligence and diplomacy: a new model for a new era. Remarks, Cipher Brief Annual Threat Conference, Sea Island, Georgia, 8 October 2023, https:www.state.gov/intelligence-and-diplomacy-a-new-model-for-a-new-era/]; Jessica Brandt. Commentary: Preempting Putin: Washington's campaign of intelligence disclosures is complicating Moscow's plans for Ukraine, Brookings, 18 February 2022, https:www.brookings.edu/articles/preempting-putin-washingtons-campaign-of-intelligence-disclosures-is-complicating-moscows-plans-for-ukraine/.

4. Mehul Srivastava. Israeli intelligence 'dismissed' detailed warning of Hamas raid. *Financial Times*, 24 November 2023, https:www.ft.com/content/277573ae-fbbc-4396-8faf-64b73ab8ed0a; Bruce Hoffman and Jacob Ware. Israel's 9/11? How Hamas terrorist attacks will change the Middle East. *War on the Rocks*, 10 October 2023, https:warontherocks.com/2023/10/israels-9-11-how-hamas-terrorist-attacks-will-change-the-middle-east/.

5. Huw Dylan and Thomas J Macguire. Secret intelligence and public diplomacy in the Ukraine war. *Survival*, 2022, vol 64, no 4, pp. 33–74.

6. Michael Herman. *Intelligence Power in Peace and War*. Cambridge: Cambridge University Press, 1996, pp. 1–15; see also Michael Herman and David Schaefer, *Intelligence Power in Practice*. Edinburgh: Edinburgh University Press, 2022.

INTELLIGENCE AND COMMUNICATION FROM THE PAST TO THE PRESENT

KGB spy Oleg Gordievsky
in disguise, London, 1990.

INTELLIGENCE, COMMUNICATION AND LEAKS: THE PERENNIAL PARADOX OF SECRET INFORMATION

Gill Bennett

Communication is key to the role of intelligence in policymaking, both in peacetime and in conflict. However professional and coordinated the system of collection and analysis, however significant the content, unless the intelligence is communicated to decision-makers it is of no value. The paradox is that it is a feature of secret intelligence – one might say part of its infrastructure – that both those collecting it and those receiving it may at times find its communication unwelcome. The information may not fit into or may contradict the assumptions on which policy has been formulated; it may raise awkward questions about the existence or reliability of sources; it may reveal uncomfortable truths or potentially cause embarrassment to allies. The temptation to delay or even withhold communication can be strong. This may produce frustration in some of those involved (with the consequent dangers of deliberate leaks), while others may be tempted to control the communication process in their own interests. Some may argue that since intelligence is normally one small part of the decision-making landscape and rarely decisive, failure to communicate it is justified if the risks of disclosure are considered significant. There are plenty of reasons for keeping secrets secret. Nevertheless, if intelligence is not communicated, the policymaking process is deficient. The fact that sometimes intelligence is available but ignored, not believed or not recognised in time does not invalidate this.

Two major international crises have recently highlighted the impact of communicated intelligence and the failure to communicate it. The Russian invasion of Ukraine in February 2022 was preceded by the United States and United Kingdom governments making public intelligence of the build-up of Russian forces and indications of the intention to invade. Although this unusual communication did not prevent the invasion, it denied an element of surprise to the aggressor and facilitated a speedy response by the international community. In respect of the Hamas attacks in Israel in October 2023, evidence has emerged that intelligence on preparations for an operation had been communicated but was discounted by those who received it, both because it did not fit with prevailing assumptions (including the primacy of technical measures) and because the source (female officers) was undervalued.

Since both these crises were ongoing at the end of 2023, and full details of the presence, absence or use of intelligence cannot be available, what follows will draw on historical examples to illustrate the importance of communication to intelligence, and some obstacles to it. First, some reasons will be considered for reluctance to communicate, or make use of, intelligence. Then some examples will be given of the ways in which intelligence can be communicated, including through the medium of leaks. Examples are drawn principally from a UK perspective and relate to civilian rather than military intelligence, obtained and communicated by agencies responsible for the collection of secret information. The piece concludes by arguing that, whatever difficulties are posed by intelligence, it is essential that those who collect it communicate it in an effective manner, and that decision-makers remain open to understanding its implications.

Why may it sometimes be considered troublesome or undesirable to communicate or be in receipt of secret intelligence? One reason is that among policymakers, interest in and appetite for intelligence varies widely. Winston Churchill, famously, was fascinated by it throughout his long political career; but other pre-Second World War decision-makers, like Stanley Baldwin and Neville Chamberlain, accepted its necessity but considered it distasteful. The exigencies of that conflict meant many members of the wartime coalition government had close relations with the much-expanded British intelligence community, something that stood Clement Attlee, as well as colleagues like Ernest Bevin and Hugh Dalton, in good stead during the 1945–51 Labour governments. Harold Wilson, as prime minister from 1964 to 1970 and 1974 to 1976, had a good relationship with the intelligence community despite a deep suspicion that they were working against him. Both he and his fellow Labour prime minister James Callaghan, in power from 1976 to 1979, would have been glad to receive useful intelligence from the Security Service (MI5) on domestic subversion, but found the service willing to collect and communicate intelligence only on individuals and organisations posing a potential threat to national security, not for political reasons.[1]

Margaret Thatcher, as prime minister, appreciated the potential value of intelligence to policymaking and understood the importance of secrecy. She was, for example, scrupulous about protecting the identity of Oleg Gordievsky, the senior KGB officer in London who was a British agent recruited by the Secret Intelligence Service (SIS/MI6) and provided information to the UK government between 1974 and his dramatic exfiltration in 1985. His intelligence was a key element in defusing the potentially dangerous situation that arose in 1983 over Able Archer, a NATO exercise in which the Supreme Allied Commander Europe sought and received authorisation to use nuclear weapons and issue dummy orders to fire tactical missiles. Gordievsky warned that although few Soviet officials with direct experience of the West took the threat of a US first strike seriously, such a fear was widespread in senior Communist Party circles. This was not understood in Washington by President Reagan and his advisers, while the Russians did not understand American intentions sufficiently.[2] In this instance, timely communication of Gordievsky's inside knowledge to Washington was clearly vital. Gordievsky's briefings also informed Thatcher's approach to Mikhail Gorbachev and the developments in the late 1980s that led to the collapse of the Warsaw Pact and Soviet Union. A less welcome communication might have been the broader insight offered by a Soviet document communicated by Gordievsky in 1985, opening with the statement 'Begin from the assumption that the United States is trying to secure a dominant position in the world regardless of the interests of other states and nations.'[3]

Thatcher was an educated consumer of intelligence, a prerequisite for the effective use of intelligence in policymaking; it is in the interests of both intelligence community and ministers that those in receipt of intelligence understand its import and limitations. In the United Kingdom, until legislation was passed between 1989 and 1996 that placed intelligence agencies on a statutory footing, the preservation of secrecy and control of information was facilitated by there being no public avowal of the components of the intelligence community and a strict maintenance of the 'neither confirm nor deny' policy. In addition to the formal machinery of the Joint Intelligence Committee, the Cabinet Secretary historically acted as

Mikhail Gorbachev poses with
Margaret Thatcher in London, 1984.

a point of liaison between the intelligence community and ministers. The addition since 2010 of the National Security Council as a forum for elucidation and discussion with ministers, together with the creation of the post of National Security Adviser, makes it even more important that all those in receipt of the intelligence, or responsible for its possible public communication, understand the information and its implications. In the 21st century both the amount and the means of transmission of intelligence have increased greatly; much of the information may be complex and technical, employing professional terms specific to the art. Technological advance has also enabled the communication, by methods that are sophisticated and hard to attribute, of disinformation and deliberately inflammatory material. In this context the education of consumers, whether officials, ministers or, when thought necessary, the public, is even more important to the effective use of intelligence.

Of course, a great deal of intelligence must necessarily remain secret, making it impossible to communicate even its major successes, such as averting a planned terrorist attack. Security and intelligence authorities are accustomed to appearing only in the news for their failures, while their successes necessarily go unheralded: indeed, publicity may hinder their work. Although the media are quick to seize on reports that a suspected terrorist was on a watch list but not under surveillance at the time of an attack, they are less ready to acknowledge that blanket surveillance is impossible, or to report that multiple plots have been detected and foiled. In 1971, Operation FOOT, involving the expulsion of 105 Soviet intelligence officers from the UK, was initiated partly because MI5 had insufficient capacity to keep tabs on the large number of identified Russian spies, and partly on the basis of intelligence communicated to MI5 by KGB double agent Oleg Lyalin. The timing and implementation of Operation FOOT was kept a close secret, with Foreign Secretary Sir Alec Douglas-Home declining to inform allies, including the Americans, in advance; he was concerned that foreknowledge might lead to leaks that would allow the Russians to take pre-emptive precautions.[4]

Nevertheless, there are times when those who collect and analyse secret intelligence are reluctant to communicate it to policymakers. This may be because of doubts about source reliability, or to protect sources; it may be because communication might expose weaknesses or failures in intelligence, risking reputational damage to the agency concerned; or because the information communicated might be embarrassing to themselves or to partners. In 1924, when the authenticity was questioned of the Zinoviev Letter, ostensibly sent by the head of the Soviet Comintern to the British Communist Party and used, when leaked to the press, to attack the Labour Party, SIS reacted by asserting – falsely – that it had 'undoubted proof' the letter was genuine and knew all the details of its transmission. SIS, like other parts of the secret intelligence community, expected such an assertion to be accepted without question. As the assistant commissioner of Scotland Yard, Sir Wyndham Childs, told an investigator, 'under no circumstances' could he question the authenticity of a document communicated by SIS's parent department, the Foreign Office (FO), since 'their opinion must overweigh that of any other living person, otherwise the Secret Service would be an impossibility'.[5] Because it is so important that intelligence disseminated to ministers has been checked, assessed and authenticated as far as is possible, decisions on when and how much to communicate are necessarily sensitive and may be finely balanced.

Another example of when intelligence was not communicated to ministers, with damaging results, was the 'Frogman' incident of 1956. An operation to send a diver to inspect the hull of a visiting Soviet ship ended in disaster with the death of Commander 'Buster' Crabb, as well as a certain amount of public scandal and a Whitehall investigation. Both SIS and the Naval Intelligence Division had considered the Crabb mission to be a low-risk venture that would not be detected – a misplaced confidence, meaning they did not obtain proper official sanction for the operation, as emerged during the investigation led by former Cabinet Secretary Sir Edward Bridges. Then, when things turned out badly, both Admiralty and FO permanent secretaries delayed informing their ministers, each claiming it was the other's responsibility. Prime Minister Anthony Eden, who had vetoed operations during the visit of Soviet leaders to the UK, was understandably furious, but a failure of the proper channels of intelligence communication was at the root of the debacle.[6]

Sometimes decision-makers may receive intelligence that they wish had *not* been communicated, because it disrupts existing plans and upsets diplomatic relations. One example of this was in September 1945, when the defection of a Soviet cypher clerk in Ottawa revealed the existence of an extensive Soviet espionage network operating on the North American continent. Igor Gouzenko's evidence was impossible to ignore, but its communication came at what the British, Canadian and US governments considered an extremely inopportune moment. At the time of the defection, less than a month after the end of the war against Japan, the participation of the Soviet Union – a member of the victorious Grand Alliance – in peacemaking (including planning for the future of occupied Germany) and in new multilateral organisations like the United Nations was both desirable and necessary. Soviet negotiators were already proving awkward interlocutors in international fora, without adding allegations of espionage into the mix.

The news communicated by Gouzenko that atomic secrets had been passed to Moscow by Soviet agents like British physicist Alan Nunn May was particularly unwelcome. President Harry Truman, adamant that the United States should now control nuclear technology, had hoped to dangle the carrot of limited access to atomic secrets before Soviet leader Josef Stalin as an incentive to co-operative behaviour. (Neither Truman, Attlee nor Canadian premier William Lyon Mackenzie King knew at this point that Moscow had been kept fully informed of nuclear developments from the inception, through Soviet agents.) Truman and his Secretary of State, James Byrnes, were reluctant to act, and although Attlee and Bevin inclined more to the view that spies named by Gouzenko should be arrested, diplomatic wrangling between London, Ottawa and Washington prevented information on the case from being made public until February 1946, when the story was leaked to the press and the Canadian government felt forced to set up a Royal Commission of Inquiry.[7] Echoes of this deep reluctance of governments, nearly 80 years ago, to communicate inconvenient intelligence may perhaps be discerned in recent media reports of statements by the Canadian and US governments in late 2023 regarding alleged Indian state involvement in attempted or actual assassination of Sikh activists in North America. Sometimes, ministers would prefer *not* to communicate intelligence received, but feel that the evidence compels them to do so.

There is a footnote to the Gouzenko case relevant to the communication of intelligence. As his interrogation progressed, reports were passed from Ottawa to London and Washington through communications channels controlled by British Security Coordination (the SIS wartime organisation based in New York) and SIS itself. In London, the person responsible for circulating these reports to the FO and to MI5 was the head of SIS Section IX, responsible for countering Soviet espionage: one Kim Philby. The evidence shows how he tried to restrict – or at least delay – communication of the Gouzenko material, allowing extra time for Soviet intelligence to suspend or wind up certain operations and protect their sources, and impeding the flow of instructions to those debriefing Gouzenko.[8] Further details of how the KGB restricted certain communications in the wake of the Gouzenko episode, and of the scale of intelligence obtained by Soviet agents, were communicated by KGB archivist Vasili Mitrokhin when he was exfiltrated to the West by SIS in 1992, bringing with him an extensive archive collected over many years. When a selection of Mitrokhin's material was published in collaboration with intelligence historian Professor Christopher Andrew, the possible international repercussions of communicating intelligence on Soviet penetration of Western governments and organisations were an issue for discussion by those involved in clearing the material for publication.[9]

Another reason why intelligence agencies may hesitate to communicate their intelligence to policymakers is reluctance to tell the truth to power when the reaction may be disbelief – or worse. Giving the 'wrong' kind of intelligence to Soviet intelligence chiefs, to Politburo members or to Stalin himself, for example, could lead to losing one's job, liberty or even life. Stalin's unwillingness to believe intelligence communicated to him that did not fit his own preconceptions led him to discount British warnings of the imminent attack on the Soviet Union by Nazi Germany in 1941, as well as to undervalue intelligence received from his well-placed British agents, the so-called Cambridge Five.[10] Stalin believed that the information they provided was too good to be true and must therefore be suspect. The best intelligence in the world is useless if officials are not prepared to communicate to political leaders what they need to know rather than what fits in with existing preconceptions. But for those leaders, paranoia is a fatal impediment to communication, and the evidence suggests that an unwillingness to accept unwelcome intelligence remains prevalent in authoritarian regimes.

Despite these difficulties, timely and effective communication has on many occasions enabled intelligence to make a useful contribution to policymaking. A notable example is the so-called Zimmermann Telegram, a message sent in January 1917 by the German foreign

Kim Philby holds a press conference in London in
November 1955, after being cleared of spying
charges by Harold Macmillan.

secretary to the German ambassador in Mexico City, instructing him to propose an alliance to the Mexican president, who would attack the southern US border and acquire territory. The telegram was intercepted by the British Admiralty's signals intelligence unit, Room 40, and communicated (by a circuitous route) to Washington; its publication on 1 March 1917 contributed to the US decision to enter the First World War on the Allied side on 6 April. Naturally, the story is more complicated than this – the Berlin telegram was actually passed through American channels – but there is no doubt of its impact.[11] Another example of a significant intelligence contribution, this time from the Second World War, involves information provided by Polish intelligence to SIS on the German V-weapon programme. It enabled the 1943 raid on the research facility in Peenemünde. Although the result was delay rather than destruction of their rocket programme, the Germans were forced to move their V-weapon testing ground to Blizna in Poland, and when a complete V2 rocket fell into muddy bushes in May 1944, the Polish Home Army photographed and dismantled it, sending key parts to London.[12] General Eisenhower later acknowledged the crucial impact of the delays to the V-weapon programme in the context of the D-Day operation.

The sharing of intelligence between allies is another example of the importance of communication, in peacetime as well as during conflict. Since 1946 the Anglo-American security and intelligence partnership, later expanded into the Five Eyes to include Canada, New Zealand and Australia, has been the bedrock of Western intelligence-sharing arrangements. This includes sharing intelligence received from debriefing defectors such as Michał Goleniewski, a senior Polish intelligence officer also working for the KGB, who then became a triple agent passing information to US intelligence authorities. In 1960 US agencies shared Goleniewski's information about Soviet spies in Britain with their British colleagues, leading to the identification of the members of the Portland Spy Ring in 1961 as well as George Blake, senior SIS officer and Soviet agent. Another defector, Anatoliy Golitsyn, provided intelligence that contributed to the identification of the Cambridge Five.[13]

Sometimes governments may decide to communicate certain intelligence proactively to the public. This can turn out badly, as happened when the UK government made public information based on flawed intelligence before the 2003 invasion of Iraq. It may, however, help to pro-mote co-operation, for example following the poisoning of the Skripals in Salisbury in 2018, when communication of some intelligence, including the identity of the Russian suspects, contributed to international solidar-ity in the response to the incident.[14] Governments may also choose to communicate intelligence deliberately for other reasons: to misdirect an adversary, for example. They may also do so inadvertently: in 2007, the posthumous award of the title of Hero of the Russian Federation to George Koval revealed for the first time that Koval had been an 'illegal' operating inside the Manhattan Project in the 1940s.[15] Intelligence on past operations or on a government's policies and counter espionage strategies may also be communicated when records are declassified, such as the considerable volume of intelligence-related records trans-ferred into the public domain in the UK National Archives by MI5, GCHQ, the Foreign, Commonwealth and Development Office and the Cabinet Office.

It could be argued that leaks are just another form of intelligence com-munication. They may be deliberate or accidental, the motivation com-plex and conflicted – one person's leak may be another's breach of secrecy. Leakage through accidental disclosure may occur because of insufficient understanding of the implications. During the 1920s, two British foreign secretaries, Lord Curzon and Sir Austen Chamberlain, disclosed in Parliament, in order to justify action taken against the USSR, that the Government Code and Cypher School (the predecessor of GCHQ) had the ability to read Russian telegraphic traffic. On the latter occasion, in 1927, this led the Soviet authorities to adopt the unbreakable 'one-time pad', destroying Britain's ability to read Soviet diplomatic messages before 1939. As SIS chief Sir Hugh Sinclair complained, an important source of intelligence was thrown away needlessly 'as a measure of des-peration to bolster up a cause vital to Government'.[16]

In wartime, governments may employ leaks as an instrument of decep-tion, to misdirect the enemy or achieve a specific objective. Some opera-tions involving 'planted' documents, such as Operation Mincemeat, are well known.[17] A less familiar example took place in 1944, as part of an investigation into the leakage of documents from the British embassy in Turkey. British Ambassador Sir Hughe Knatchbull-Hugessen refused to accept that his valet, Ilyas Bazna (codenamed Cicero), was responsible for leaking documents to the Germans. To obtain proof, a fake Cabinet paper

Two men read the *South China Morning Post* carrying the story of former US spy Edward Snowden, Hong Kong, 2013.

was concocted by the chairman of the Joint Intelligence Committee and made to look authentic (including the forgery of Eden's initials by his private secretary, Pierson Dixon) and planted in the embassy, in the hope that it would provoke a German reaction confirming the source of the leak.[18]

Sometimes government officials leak intelligence. The unauthorised disclosure of documents by malign actors such as Edward Snowden, a contractor employed on the fringes of US intelligence but with extensive access, was extremely damaging. Other cases are more complex. Officials may be provoked to leak documents by frustration at government inaction, because they consider that wrongdoing is being covered up – or even because they feel the public has a right to know. A well-known example of this was the leaking to the US press in 1971 by military analyst Daniel Ellsberg of a classified Department of Defense study on decision-making in Vietnam.[19]

Though Ellsberg was prosecuted, the trial collapsed in the light of revelations about the misdeeds of the Nixon White House, and the Pentagon Papers became an important source on US policy in Vietnam. A rather different but related British example concerned the leakage in April 1984 by civil servant Clive Ponting of documents concerning the sinking of the Argentine ship ARA *General Belgrano* during the Falklands conflict in 1982. Tam Dalyell MP had alleged that instructions to attack the *Belgrano* were given despite a peace settlement being on the table; indeed, he alleged it was sunk in order to prevent such a settlement. This was untrue, but statements made in Parliament in response by the prime minister and defence secretary, based on confusing initial reports, were partially inaccurate and were not withdrawn or corrected, fuelling suspicion of a cover-up. Ponting, who worked at the Ministry of Defence, believed that the material was not sensitive and that there should be full disclosure to Parliament in answer to Dalyell and others. He sent copies of documents to Dalyell and was prosecuted under the Official Secrets Act, but he argued that his actions had been in the public interest and was acquitted.[20] Sir Lawrence Freedman, official historian of the Falklands conflict, noted that the whole affair arose from the different methods of communication used for classified and unclassified material, commenting that 'reluctance to acknowledge what was already in the public domain was rationalised in terms of "political credibility" and the tendency for each answer simply to raise more questions'.[21]

All governments abhor leaks of their own information, and when one occurs an investigation will be set in train. In Britain, such investigations have rarely resulted in the identification of a culprit (indeed, historically, the most common source of leaks has been 10 Downing Street itself). But leaks clearly have the potential to inflict considerable damage, particularly when they are employed by a hostile organisation or power. The increasing incidence and sophistication of cyber warfare is a force multiplier of the effects of the unauthorised communication of information. A number of Russian 'hack and leak' operations have been detected, for example. For a more positive interpretation, however, one might give the last word on leaks to Professor John Ferris, official historian of GCHQ, who pointed out: 'All leaks after 2000…suggest that GCHQ's success in diplomatic Comint [communications intelligence] during the internet age has reached the highest levels in history, providing much first-rate material on first-rate issues.'[22]

As noted earlier, intelligence is rarely, though sometimes, decisive as an element in policymaking, and indeed on some major long-term strategic decisions it may have little effect. But it is nevertheless a piece of the jigsaw, and the picture is incomplete without it. Whatever the doubts and difficulties, it is vital that those who collect and analyse intelligence continue to communicate it in a timely and effective manner, and that decision-makers are open to receiving it and make the necessary efforts to understand its implications. They should not emulate Harold Macmillan, who as prime minister was exasperated by a succession of British 'spy scandals' in the early 1960s and said, when informed of the arrest in 1961 of Admiralty clerk John Vassall for supplying secrets to Russia, that he was 'not at all pleased. When my gamekeeper shoots a fox, he doesn't go and hang it up outside the Master of Foxhounds' drawing room; he buries it out of sight…Why the devil did you "catch" him?'[23]

1. See Christopher Andrew, *The Defence of the Realm: the Authorized History of MI5*. London: Penguin, 2009, Section E.

2. For an insider's account of these events, see Gordon Barrass, *The Great Cold War: a Journey Through the Hall of Mirrors*. Redwood City, CA: Stanford University Press, 2009.

3. Quoted in Kevin P Riehle, *Russian Intelligence: a Case-Based Study of Russian Services and Missions Past and Present*. Bethesda, MD: National Intelligence University Press, 2022, p. 105. A good account of Mrs Thatcher's appreciation of the intelligence communicated by Gordievsky can be found in Charles Moore, *Margaret Thatcher: the Authorized Biography, Volume Two: Everything She Wants*. London: Allen Lane, 2015.

4. See Gill Bennett, *Six Moments of Crisis: Inside British Foreign Policy*. Oxford: Oxford University Press, 2013, ch 5.

5. Gill Bennett. *The Zinoviev Letter: the Conspiracy that Never Dies*. Oxford: Oxford University Press, 2018, pp. 83–4.

6. Documentation on the Frogman operation and its consequences has been transferred to the National Archives (TNA) as part of the Cabinet Secretary's Secret and Personal archive, in files CAB 301/121ff. Further detail can be found in Michael S Goodman, Covering up spying in the 'Buster' Crabb affair. *International History Review*, vol 30, no 4, December 2008, pp. 768–784.

7. See Gill Bennett, The CORBY case: the defection of Igor Gouzenko, September 1945, in *From World War to Cold War: the Records of the Foreign Office Permanent Under-Secretary's Department 1939–51*, https:issuu.com/fcohistorians/docs/pusdessays. (CORBY was the codename for the Gouzenko case.) On the nuclear aspect see Michael D Gordin, *Red Cloud at Dawn: Truman, Stalin, and the End of the Atomic Monopoly*. New York: Farrar, Straus and Giroux, 2009.

8. See Keith Jeffery, *MI6: the History of the Secret Intelligence Service 1909–49*. London: Bloomsbury, 2010, p. 656.

9. Christopher Andrew and Vasili Mitrokhin. *The Mitrokhin Archive*, vol 1, *The KGB in Europe and the West*; vol 2, *The KGB in the World*. London: Penguin, 1999 and 2005.

10. David Murphy. *What Stalin Knew: the Enigma of Barbarossa*. New Haven: Yale University Press, 2005. There are many accounts of the Cambridge Five (Guy Burgess, Donald Maclean, Kim Philby, John Cairncross and Anthony Blunt), but for an interesting Russian overview see Yuri Modin, *My Five Cambridge Friends*. London: Headline, 1994.

11. For an authoritative account see Peter Freeman, The Zimmermann Telegram revisited: a reconciliation of the primary sources. Cryptologia, vol 30, no 2, 2006, pp. 98–150.

12. See chapters 45 and 48 in Tessa Stirling, Daria Nalecz and Tadeusz Dubicki (eds.), *The Report of the Anglo-Polish Historical Committee, Volume 1, Intelligence Cooperation between Poland and Great Britain during World War II*. London: Vallentine Mitchell, 2005.

13. Andrew, *Defence of the Realm*, Section D, ch 6 and 9.

14. See Mark Urban, *The Skripal Files: Putin, Poison and the New Spy War* (rev. edn.). London: Pan, 2019.

15. Riehle, *Russian Intelligence*, p. 18.

16. An account of both episodes can be found in Gill Bennett, *Churchill's Man of Mystery: Desmond Morton and the World of Intelligence*. London: Routledge, 2006, pp. 64, 94–5.

17. Ewen Montagu. *The Man Who Never Was: the Remarkable Story of Operation Mincemeat*. Cheltenham: The History Press, 2021, first published 1953. For a related episode see The man who was: the 'Clamorgan Affair' and the origins of Operation Mincemeat in FCO Historians, *From World War to Cold War*, pp. 49–59, https:issuu.com/fcohistorians/docs/pusdessays.

18. See *The Cicero Papers*, FCO Historians, 2005, https:issuu.com/fcohistorians/docs/hpdfba_7.

19. Ellsberg's book, *Secrets: a Memoir of Vietnam and the Pentagon Papers*, was reissued by Penguin in 2003.

20. Ponting published his account of the episode in *The Right to Know: the Inside Story of the Belgrano Affair*. London: Sphere, 1985.

21. Sir Lawrence Freedman. *The Official History of the Falklands Campaign, Volume II, War and Diplomacy*. London: Routledge, 2005, pp. 736ff.

22. John Ferris. *Behind the Enigma: the Authorised History of GCHQ, Britain's Secret Cyber-Intelligence Agency*. London: Bloomsbury, 2020, p. 499.

23. Andrew, *Defence of the Realm*, p. 493.

Iraqi prime minister General Abdul-Karim
Qasim at a function in Baghdad, 1961.

BRITAIN'S JOINT INTELLIGENCE COMMITTEE AND WARNING IN THE 1960s: THE CASE STUDIES OF KUWAIT AND CZECHOSLOVAKIA

Michael Goodman

The Joint Intelligence Committee (JIC) is one of the longest-serving committees in Whitehall, the centre of UK government decision-making. Its origins can be traced back to a decision in 1936 to remedy the lack of coordination within the secret world. The 1960s JIC was a committee at the top of its game, operating at the interface of intelligence and policy, but also intelligence assessment and covert action. Chaired by a succession of high-flying Foreign Office diplomats, its weekly meetings were attended by the heads of the intelligence agencies, including the domestic Security Service (MI5), the foreign Secret Intelligence Service (SIS) and the Signals Intelligence agency, the Government Communications Headquarters (GCHQ), as well as the chief of the Defence Intelligence Staff and senior policy officials from the Ministry of Defence, Foreign Office, Colonial Office and elsewhere as required.

The changes instigated in 1957 had seen the JIC move into the Cabinet Office, a change designed to reflect the enlarging scope of the JIC in subject matter but also a broadening out of customer departments – no longer was intelligence simply the preserve of defence. In practice, this meant the JIC spent as much time looking at military matters as it did looking at political, scientific or economic ones. The focus of the Committee in the early 1960s reflected the demands of the Cold War, which remained the number one priority, while also monitoring Soviet influence and the spread of Communism around the globe.

Yet from the 1950s onwards, other issues rose in priority too. In particular, Britain's retreat from empire and its removal of influence from east of Suez led to a rise in localised skirmishes which threatened British interests. Monitoring these events and watching out for signs of unrest and the first stirrings of a crisis became the mainstay of the JIC's work.[1]

The two examples considered in this short paper reflect these concerns and interests. They highlight the central role of the JIC, sitting at the top of the intelligence pyramid, looking down upon a hugely expensive intelligence community, setting requirements and assessing performance, while also looking upwards towards policymakers, producing an array of intelligence assessments. The JIC was (and remains) defined by its deliberate mixture of intelligence and policymaking officials, and the fact that this consensus lies at the heart of everything it does. The two examples are intentionally contrasting: the first considers what we might think of as an intelligence success; whereas the second most certainly is not. In contemplating the details, the paper will conclude with a consideration of what these examples tell us about the study of intelligence success and failure.

Kuwait: 1961

The first stirrings of trouble began in 1958 in Iraq. The ruling royal family was overthrown in a bloodthirsty revolution. The replacement military government, led by Brigadier Abd Qasim, wasted no time in publicly calling for the absorption of Kuwait into the new Iraqi Republic. For Britain this was hugely problematic. Not only did a defensive 'protection' agreement with the Kuwaiti ruler exist (and had done since 1899), but by the late 1950s Britain was getting the majority of its oil from Kuwait.[2] Qasim himself was considered by the JIC to be a 'sincere and upright idealist, but with distinctly fanatical leanings'.[3] That view was tempered somewhat over the next 12–24 months, but the UK government maintained a keen interest in what was happening in the region.[4]

A JIC paper in April 1959 had highlighted how the intelligence machinery could expect to receive 'not less than four days, warning of an assembly force' within Iraq. This assessment would become critical. The military Chiefs of Staff had concluded that if Britain waited until the Iraqis invaded Kuwait before intervening, it would be futile to think they could be removed easily or quickly. Importantly for the JIC, the challenge was to have sufficiently good intelligence to be assured of Iraqi intentions, but crucially to have this information prior to any formal Kuwaiti assistance being requested, so plans could be put in place.[5]

Monitoring developments through 1960, the JIC increasingly took a view that an attack, despite all the rhetoric, was unlikely. Nonetheless, diplomatic planning and military preparations continued, unsurprising given Britain's reliance on Kuwaiti oil and its defensive commitment. The formal granting of independence to Kuwait in the summer of 1961 annulled the 1899 agreement, but it did not change the military assurance in case of attack.

In late June 1961, the Defence Committee decided to increase readiness levels. A few days earlier Qasim had publicly announced that Kuwait was part of Iraq. Taken together with what else was known, the JIC's immediate response was to step up its readiness level. On 30 June, British ministers met and discussed what was known about the situation. The response was to instruct British forces to land and take up positions in Kuwait, a move that had been formally requested by the Kuwaiti leader.[6] Operation Vantage, as it was known, swung into action with approximately 7,000 British troops sent out, with a further 3,000 held in readiness for deployment.[7]

While frantic assessments went back and forth, in Iraq itself little was apparently happening. The initial assessment in early July was that any possible Iraqi action would take place in mid-July to coincide with the anniversary of the Iraqi Revolution. Within a few days, however, that view was moderated and the JIC could conclude that such an attack was now 'unlikely'. By 20 July the JIC downgraded the security alert.[8]

A month later, in its first detailed assessment since the deployment of troops, the JIC noted that while there was no evidence that an Iraqi invasion would take place, nonetheless the possibility could not be excluded simply because Qasim 'is under some pressure to take positive action'. Writing again a few months later, the JIC remained concerned at the potential threat posed by Iraq, even if no evidence of any specifics could be discerned. The British troops departed Kuwait in October 1961, to be replaced by a contingent from the Arab League. The crisis was not over, even if responsibility had been passed on.

The case study of the Iraqi threat to Kuwait in the summer of 1961 highlights a number of issues. Firstly, at one level it is an example of an intelligence success in as much as there was a clear intelligence requirement for information; the assessment was made quickly and all those who read it agreed with its sentiments. It also had the desired effect in the political and military response. Yet on the other hand it highlights the difficulties of making an assessment and potentially forestalling whatever the feared event was, with the result that nothing happened. The lack of an Iraqi attack, therefore, might be down to the immediate and substantial British military response; or it might be down to the fact that they were never going to attack in the first place. No evidence is available to conclusively show what Qasim had in mind. For the JIC, the question was one of risk: if the threat remained yet no explicit action was expected, surely the government should know and be allowed to make its own policy? More than anything, the example of Kuwait in the summer of 1961 highlighted the challenge of acting pre-emptively based on intelligence. That would be very different seven years later.

Czechoslovakia: 1968

One event in 1968 served to highlight the JIC's warning role. The JIC had always produced assessments of Soviet intentions towards both Western and Eastern Europe. In September 1967 it issued the latest revision to its regular paper, 'Warning of Soviet attack on the West'. As the Committee had concluded over the preceding two decades, the paper began with the unequivocal view that 'the Russians will not deliberately initiate general war'. This conclusion was not based on any hard and fast intelligence, but rather a reading of the Russians' 'political and military posture and the disadvantages to them of taking such action'. The three elements to this assessment – gauging intent, monitoring capabilities and reading the Russian mindset – would be central to the intelligence process in assessments of the Czechoslovak crisis the following year. Attempts to assess all three aspects, as the JIC readily conceded, was tremendously difficult; and intelligence of one could not be used to impute another.[9]

The first stirrings of crisis in Czechoslovakia began with the economy, specifically in attempts to liberalise it from the strictures of central Communist planning. In the spring of 1968 Alexander Dubček, First Secretary of the Czechoslovakian Communist Party, took things further with a widespread change in the senior echelons of his party: the publication of the 'Action Programme', which referred to the necessity of reforming the entire political system in Czechoslovakia. For the leaders of the Soviet bloc, this was a step too far. Beginning in late March, the leaders of East Germany, Bulgaria, Hungary, Poland and the USSR had a series of meetings to discuss Dubček and to pressure Leonid Brezhnev, General Secretary of the Communist Party of the Soviet Union, to do something

Second Battalion troops from Cyprus go about
their duties watched by Kuwaiti officials, 1961.

to bring him under control. The four satellite states urged the Soviet Union to intervene to halt the Czech liberalisation.

Initially this pressure was to be felt in a series of Warsaw Pact military exercises, culminating in a large command post exercise on Czechoslovakian territory in late June 1968. Prior to the start of deployments, there had been no Soviet troops based on Czechoslovakian soil. By its culmination, the military manoeuvres were to result in the arrival of over 25,000 troops. Most but by no means all of the Warsaw Pact forces withdrew from Czechoslovakian territory by 19 July, with the final divisions leaving on 3 August. These moves were complemented by a widespread disinformation campaign by the Soviet security and intelligence service, the KGB.[10]

Monitoring the political and military developments, the JIC concluded that 'while the possibility of Soviet military intervention cannot be altogether excluded, we consider it unlikely'. In the absence of direct intelligence, the JIC could only apply its own logic to the situation: in hindsight, it would be a classic case of applying transferred judgement and mirror imaging.

While Brezhnev had the means to crush the Czechoslovakian counter-revolution, there was no intelligence to suggest one way or another whether he would do so. The JIC's conclusion, mirrored by the Foreign Office, was that a military response was a less viable option on the grounds that it would generate a negative reaction worldwide. What the JIC did not consider in its assessment was whether Brezhnev would be forced to choose this option and disregard the possible worldwide reaction, given that reasserting control was more important.

In late July 1968 Dubček was given one final chance to stop the 'counter-revolution'. Meanwhile, new Warsaw Pact exercises began. The troops that had taken part in the exercises of the previous month in Czechoslovakia had been withdrawn, though they remained stationed around the periphery of the border. Joining them were a number of additional troops; the result was a vast array of military force concentrated around Czechoslovakia. For the JIC the military exercises were part of the continuing war of nerves, a means of exerting psychological pressure on Dubček.

The final decision to invade was taken by the Politburo on 17 August 1968. Preparations were made to start the attack the following day. The timing was significant: it was a Sunday, when Soviet military activity was normally light; in addition, 18 August was Soviet Air Force Day,

A young Czech girl shouts 'Ivan go home!' at
Russian soldiers sitting on tanks in the streets
of Prague, 1968.

traditionally a holiday within the air force. The invasion itself began at 20:30 local time on Tuesday 20 August. Within a few hours, a quarter of a million Soviet Bloc troops crossed the border and marched into Czechoslovakia. The Czechoslovakian army, whose leadership had been changed by Dubček months earlier, offered no resistance. Dubček himself, together with several other leaders, was arrested and transported to Moscow. Within 24 hours the Soviet Union had achieved the total military occupation of Czechoslovakia, and within no time the liberal changes wrought by Dubček were reversed, with Czechoslovakia returning to its former position as a faithful ally of the Soviet Union.[11]

Immediately afterwards, the JIC conducted a post-mortem into what had gone wrong. The JIC found it tremendously difficult to grasp the perspective of those in the Kremlin, judging that the likely public response would be too damaging to allow for an invasion to be a realistic prospect. This, together with the assessment that Brezhnev's overall outlook prioritised détente with the West, led to a belief that Russia taking a military option would be unlikely. Thus, the JIC underestimated the lengths to which the Soviet Union would go to maintain its control of the Communist bloc in Eastern Europe.

A separate study by the Ministry of Defence concluded that if evidence of military capabilities had been considered in isolation, then the novel and unusual nature of this mobilisation would have suggested that this was more than a troop exercise. But this view was tempered by a judgement of the Soviets' political intentions.[12]

Conclusion

These two examples highlight different aspects of the JIC's warning function, but together emphasise that its most important role was just that: to provide warning. To predict any event, several key questions need to be addressed: what, when, why, where and how. As a body predominantly focused on strategy, the JIC faced an unenviable task: analysts had to issue a strategic warning far enough in advance of the feared event for officials to have an opportunity to take preventive action, yet with the credibility to motivate them to do so. Perhaps even more difficult is to provide a detailed, tactical warning, not least given the limitations of intelligence.

The JIC had to be satisfied by three factors to conclude that a country was preparing for an act of aggression:

1. that the country would have the political will to undertake such action;
2. that military action would achieve a desired political end; and
3. that specific military preparations to that end had already begun.

But high-level, reliable intelligence on these was almost always lacking, so analysis and interpretation became vital.

Consideration must also be given to the JIC itself in assessing its performance. One underlying issue is that of consensus: the JIC system was predicated on producing a unified, agreed report, yet it was not always possible to reach this consensus, and at times that can – and did – lead to a report with the lowest common denominator, often offering the blandest, vaguest assessment; another outcome is that a paper might be issued in the JIC's name, but not everyone was as convinced as the majority. Related to this, and something Lord Butler commented upon much later in his report on Iraqi weapons of mass destruction, is the tone of the assessments themselves. The majority of the JIC's strategic assessments during the Cold War were so equivocal in content and tone that any number of events would have been considered possible; rarely were explicit statements or points of view expressed.

Rather than trying to end with any prophetic conclusions, a final word comes from a quote from one of the Foreign Office's research analysts, who worked there for the majority of the first half of the 20th century:

> Year after year the worriers and fretters would come to me with awful predictions of the outbreak of war. I denied it each time. I was only wrong twice.
>
> It's just a shame that those two errors were in 1914 and 1939.

1. For more see R J Aldrich, R Cormac and M S Goodman, *Spying on the World: the Declassified Documents of the Joint Intelligence Committee, 1936–2013.* Edinburgh: Edinburgh University Press, 2014.

2. N J Ashton. A microcosm of decline: British loss of nerve and military intervention in Jordan and Kuwait, 1958 and 1961. *Historical Journal*, vol 40, no 4, 1997, pp. 1069–83.

3. National Archives. CAB 158/33, JIC(58)76(Final). The immediate outlook in Iraq, 5 August 1958.

4. R A Mobley. Gauging the threat to Kuwait in the 1960s. *CIA Studies in Intelligence*, autumn/winter 2001, pp. 19–31.

5. National Archives. CAB 158/36, JIC(59)28(Final). The military threat from Iraq to Kuwait by March 1960, 30 April 1959.

6. N Ashton. Britain and the Kuwaiti crisis, 1961. *Diplomacy and Statecraft*, vol 9, no 1, 1998, pp. 163–81.

7. M M Alani. *Operation Vantage: British Military Intervention in Kuwait 1961.* Surbiton: LAAM, 1990.

8. National Archives. CAB 159/35, JIC(61), 38th meeting, 20 July 1961.

9. For an overview, see P Cradock, *Know Your Enemy: How the Joint Intelligence Committee Saw the World.* London: John Murray, 2002.

10. G Bischof, S Karner and P Ruggenthaler (eds.). *The Prague Spring and the Warsaw Pact Invasion of Czechoslovakia in 1968.* Lanham, MD: Lexington Books, 2009.

11. J Valenta. *Soviet Intervention in Czechoslovakia, 1968: Anatomy of a Decision.* London: Johns Hopkins University Press, 1991.

12. National Archives. PREM 13/1994, Intelligence warning, contained in J Mayne [MoD] to D. Maitland [PPS to Foreign Secretary], 26 August 1968.

André Dewavrin, codenamed Colonel
Passy, leader of Free French intelligence
under General Charles de Gaulle.

SHARING IN SECRET: INTELLIGENCE LIAISON AND INTERNATIONAL DIPLOMACY

Matthew Hefler

The relationships between allied intelligence services – and between allied intelligence officers – are important state-to-state relationships within international diplomacy.[1] They are also some of the most secret. Take for instance the 'Five Eyes' intelligence alliance, led by the United States and the United Kingdom, and the way its existence and operation can have an impact on strategy and diplomacy across governments and across the world. It shapes things like the West's ability to effectively support Ukraine in its resistance to Russian aggression, or efforts by Canadian and allied leaders to allege the involvement of the Indian government in an assassination on Canadian soil.[2] Or consider the frequent diplomacy undertaken by William Burns, Director of the Central Intelligence Agency (CIA), both around the war in Ukraine and Israel's military actions against Hamas.[3] Yet despite their importance to international affairs and relations, intelligence relationships are some of the most inaccessible aspects of government activity. Like intelligence material itself – which is classified and released to the public later than other official documents, if it is released at all[4] – details around intelligence liaison with foreign states can be guarded more jealously than other forms of diplomatic and strategic engagement. This is despite the fact that clandestine relationships can have an impact on the highest levels of policy and security.

This paper is about the relationships between the intelligence services of foreign states, and about how intelligence liaison can influence national policy and even international diplomacy. It uses historical examples and some important archival evidence to examine intelligence relationships and identify some of the key aspects in their development and maintenance. It argues that while many factors shape successful intelligence relationships, three important aspects stand out: circumstances, culture and personal relations. This is particularly true when considering the way clandestine relationships can influence domestic policy and international developments. Declassified intelligence material can illuminate the way relationships between allied intelligence services and officers can shape wider strategy and statecraft. This paper concludes by drawing historical insights with the present, shedding light on what sort of questions must be asked about contemporary intelligence relationships, like those developing between the Western allies and Ukraine.

A real-world example can help frame intelligence relationships. On Christmas Eve 2003, General Michael Hayden, director of the National Security Agency (NSA), the American signals intelligence agency, called his counterpart in Britain, David Pepper, director of the UK's Government Communications Headquarters (GCHQ).[5] The NSA had acquired information which suggested that Washington DC might soon face a devastating terrorist attack, one that would disable NSA headquarters in nearby Maryland. Hayden said to Pepper: 'David…I've told my liaison to your office that should there be catastrophic loss at Fort Meade, we are turning the functioning of the American [signals intelligence] system over to GCHQ.' Fortunately, the attack never came, but the anecdote is still striking.

People interested in international affairs are aware of the concept of the Anglo–American 'Special Relationship'. Some again would agree that, if it exists anywhere in reality, it exists in the closeness of the intelligence relationship between these two powers.[6] Activities around signals intelligence (SIGINT) are some of the most secretive pursuits in which modern states engage. The idea that two sovereign states, no matter how close, could collaborate in these areas – and so closely that if one side were to disappear, the other would be expected and permitted to perform SIGINT functions for the disabled partner – is nothing short of remarkable. Yet if the Hayden–Pepper call speaks to the profound closeness of the US–UK partnership, it is a closeness that was built over time through institutions, through experience, and through the forging of lasting professional and personal relationships. In other words, through trust.[7]

While many are familiar with the Anglo–American relationship, many are less familiar with the incredible amount of intelligence Western allies are sharing with Ukraine to help that country defend itself from Russian aggression. As noted by other authors in this collection, allied intelligence services had already played a notable role around the start of the conflict.

In the run-up to the invasion, allied intelligence agencies, especially in the USA and UK, were employed in efforts around 'public diplomacy', declassifying intelligence material almost in real time to check Russian actions and contest the information space.[8] Former White House press secretary Jen Psaki said in March 2022 that 'the United States had been sharing real-time intelligence assisting Kyiv's defensive posture, to "inform and develop their military response to Russia's invasion"'.[9] Other reports suggest information had been provided on Russian troop movements, 'intercepted communications about their military plans' and even that 'foreign intelligence helped the Ukrainians target and sink the Russian cruiser *Moskva*'.[10] Reporting in the *New York Times* has shed light on the close co-operation developing between Ukrainian intelligence and allied services, especially the CIA.[11] The extent of this sharing with a country outside the Five Eyes alliance speaks not only to the urgency felt by Western allies over Ukraine, but highlights the value of these intelligence relationships themselves.

To explore these issues, this essay examines two important intelligence relationships from the time of the Second World War: that between Britain and the United States of America, and that between Britain and France. To do this, the paper uses records from intelligence archives of the UK and the USA, including declassified British SIGINT, which provide powerful snapshots of these relationships – and the place of circumstances, culture and personal relations in their development and maintenance.

Circumstances

The British–American intelligence relationship was formed in the special circumstances of the Second World War. Collaboration against the Axis powers included sharing the most secret intelligence material of the war – codenamed Ultra – or intelligence gleaned from solving the German Enigma cipher machine, a major accomplishment which, while an Allied effort, was achieved by the British at Bletchley Park.[12] Close co-operation over such sensitive material, in such difficult circumstances, helped to establish the most intimate intelligence-sharing relationship in the world.

Yet the US–UK intelligence relationship was not pre-ordained. Special and sometimes monumental circumstances were required to bring the Allies together. Prior to the fall of France in June 1940, Franco–British intelligence co-operation looked set to develop an intimacy on much the same lines as the Anglo–American relationship.[13] And this mattered. Personal relationships that had developed in the interwar years reappeared during the war and had important impacts. Consider for instance the way co-operation between leading British and French intelligence figures continued, at least on 'personal levels', even after France signed an armistice with Germany and British intelligence was, for security reasons, forced to wall up its operations against its recent allies. An important case was the continuing British contact with Major Gustave Bertrand, head of French cryptography, who continued to work against Axis codes in secret even after the armistice.[14]

The importance of circumstances was underscored again in the wartime struggle for mastery of the French secret services between, on the one hand, the Bureau Central de Renseignements et d'Action (BCRA), the Free French intelligence service established by General Charles de Gaulle under the command of the young captain André Dewavrin, or 'Colonel Passy', and establishment figures from the interwar Deuxième Bureau, like General Louis Rivet, on the other. As this contest reached a climax over 1943–4, British services as a whole were cautious about their involvement. By then, their fighting allegiances had them alongside Passy's service, with its links to the Resistance groups inside France, but many British leaders had respect and long personal histories with men like Rivet and the pre-war counterintelligence chief Colonel Paul Paillole.[15] Circumstances did lead some to try and massage the outcome. Declassified SIGINT of BCRA correspondence reveals that some MI5 and MI6 officers made strong efforts to see that, no matter what happened in the 'intelligence war', Paillole would keep his place as head of counterintelligence – a clear case of circumstances and personal relationships coming together, and in a struggle with real implications for the future of French intelligence and of Franco–British relations.[16]

Culture
This framing of events underscores the importance of circumstances in shaping the development of intelligence relationships: in this case, the role of wartime defeats in warping Franco–British co-operation and setting the stage for Anglo–American collaboration. Yet other factors are

significant as well. Culture, in both national and institutional forms, plays a significant role. The establishment of the US–UK relationship required a steep learning curve. John Ferris, the doyen of SIGINT history, has shown us the complex manner in which co-operation developed. In contrast to other areas, the British remained the stronger partner in the realm of SIGINT throughout the war. Ferris argues that this fact, along with the regular jealousies and personality clashes inherent in bureaucracies, could contribute to irritation and misunderstandings.[17]

Primary materials at the National Archives II in College Park, Maryland offer insight into the US view of how the relationship took shape. The Special Research Histories (SRH) of the NSA help preserve vital institutional records around things as fundamental as the development of relations with the British. These documents underscore the role of national and organisational culture, or how cultural differences shaped working relationships. These differences were not aesthetic; they had a real impact on the strengths and weaknesses of the collaboration. This can be seen in daily functioning, *in just getting along.* For instance, American officers recognised that Brits trained differently. Lots of this took place – perhaps unsurprisingly – over tea; informal conversations about unconventional work. This was not sufficiently formal or comprehensive for some American officers.[18]

The author of one SRH argued that: 'Besides getting along with the British, the Americans had to understand them.'[19] Assessments underscored the importance of having liaison officers who could relate to or work well with the cultures in question. Yet even the close cultural background of Americans and Brits was not enough to stop misunderstandings, even over simple things. One example was the confusion that resulted from the way a British officer characterised the quantity of fuel stored at a depot. The officer noted that a certain amount of fuel was 'disposed of' at the depot. Unbeknownst to his American counterpart, the British officer had meant the fuel was 'held at the depot', not 'discarded by it'.[20] These sorts of miscommunications may appear small, but they had significant implications. If instances like these were plentiful enough, and important enough, to feature prominently in this Special Research History, even among partners with as close a cultural background as the British and Americans shared, then this underscores the significance of culture to the working of intelligence

relationships more broadly. In fact, another SRH highlights the importance of navigating cultural differences to successful intelligence
co-operation – officers who could do so were singled out for recogni-
tion.[21]

Personal relations

Declassified records highlight the importance of circumstances in setting the stage for intelligence relationships and the way culture can
facilitate or obstruct their functioning. But an even more prominent
aspect of intelligence liaison tends to emerge from the archival evidence: the role of personal relationships between allied intelligence
officers. This is significant, in part because just as the secret work of
intelligence officers has been concealed through its covert nature and
the protection of the relevant archives up to today, so have the personal
relationships formed in the course of this work been obscured through
levels of classification and archival inaccessibility. Today, however,
newly declassified intelligence records underscore the importance to
intelligence liaison of relationships between intelligence officers. Still
further, these give an indication of how clandestine relationships built
on intimacy and trust have the potential to affect diplomatic relations at
high levels and wider international diplomacy itself.

To explore these connections, this essay looks at two important pieces
of communications intelligence, or COMINT, a subsection of SIGINT,
from the UK National Archives at Kew. They are two cables sent by the
Gaullist intelligence services, the BCRA, and subsequently intercepted
and decrypted (or 'solved') by the UK's Government Code and Cipher
School (GC&CS), the forerunner of today's GCHQ. One intercepted
cable highlights the importance of international diplomacy to intelligence work. The other shows how the relationship can go the other way;
how clandestine intelligence relationships have the capacity to influence
high policy and international diplomacy.

These messages are a special form of COMINT, because by being the
intercepted correspondence of the BCRA, they were also the intercepted
correspondence of Allied intelligence services. This was incredibly sensitive material. Major General Stewart Menzies, or 'C', the wartime head
of the British Secret Intelligence Service, knew spying on allies was some
of the most sensitive work conducted by the British secret services.[22]

Major General Sir Stewart Menzies, head of the
British Secret Intelligence Service during the
Second World War, with his bride Pamela, 1932.

They were still more sensitive given the delicate nature of the wartime relations between Britain and France, and especially between Prime Minister Winston Churchill and General Charles de Gaulle. The latter relationship was stormy to say the least, with the result that Franco–British relations were frequently near breaking point at important moments during the war.

One of the most tense periods came in December 1943, when the Comité français de libération nationale (CFLN) made the decision to arrest a number of officials who had served the Vichy France regime. This prompted an explosion among the Allies because, as some of the arrested men had made efforts to facilitate the Allied invasion of French North Africa in 1942, Churchill and the US president, Franklin Roosevelt, felt they owed the men a personal debt.[23] Though the diplomatic fallout would eventually be quashed, intelligence files give a sense of how intelligence relationships helped sustain state-to-state relations, even when top-level relations were in crisis.

On 23 December, in a cable that would be intercepted by British intelligence, the Free French intelligence leader Colonel Passy told his subordinate in London: 'A great political crisis is breaking.'[24] The British and American ambassadors had 'made a joint effort' to secure the release of the arrested officials. However, despite the threat of a rupture in relations, 'the Committee did not give in'. But the wider diplomatic crisis was threatening intelligence co-operation. Most notably, all flights to London had been stopped. Passy had arranged for some of his people to take off from Marrakesh with some of the 'English of MI6'. Passy told his subordinate to go at once to Claude Dansey, Menzies' deputy and second in command of MI6, and 'ask him to give orders so that my staff can move easily in both directions'. And to get this done, Passy instructed him to 'emphasise my personally very friendly intentions towards him'.[25]

This first cable provides a clear sense of how the tumults of international diplomacy could derail the day-to-day operations of intelligence work. Yet more significantly here, it underscores the real importance of personal relations in intelligence liaison. Specifically, we get a glimpse of how individual relationships between Allied intelligence officers had the potential to sustain levels of state-to-state co-operation – even in adverse political conditions. Passy's detailed instructions reveal that, first, he had developed a close working relationship with Dansey, and second, that he

Lieutenant Colonel Claude Dansey, also known
as Colonel Z, assistant chief of the British Secret
Intelligence Service.

believed evoking this relationship had the power to overcome the obstacles erected by a crisis at the top of politics.

The first intercepted BCRA cable is a notable piece of archival evidence: a message from a French intelligence chief that underscores the way intelligence liaison can be impacted upon by diplomatic crises, and the role of personal relations in that equation. The next cable examines how intelligence relations have the capacity to shape strategy and statecraft, and the role of trust between intelligence officers within that process.

This second cable is an even more extraordinary historical artefact. It is again from the intercepted correspondence of the BCRA, by now renamed the Direction générale des Études et Recherches (DGER). It is a message sent from French intelligence in London to the Gaullist leaders of the French Secret Service in now liberated Paris; so from one of Passy's lieutenants back to Colonel Passy. The transmission was sent on 7 February 1945, as the war was finally nearing its end, and its importance can be seen from the first line: 'Absolutely secret. Very important to not distribute.'[26]

The messenger explained that, the day before, he had had 'a long conversation with General Menzies' ('C', the head of MI6). The timing was critical: Menzies had opted to offer these confidences on 6 February 1945, just at the time when, in faraway Crimea, the leaders of the UK, the USA and the USSR – the Big Three – were engaged in the Yalta Conference, deciding much of the end of the war.

At this critical time, Menzies addressed a number of issues that were front and centre for French diplomacy, strategy and intelligence. These included the occupation of Germany and whether France would receive an occupation zone, as well as Allied relations with the Soviet Union and the place of intelligence in those relations. By default, these topics address the fears of future Russian intentions that had gripped senior levels of British and American intelligence and military services. It is clear that in making these comments, Menzies wanted to shape French diplomatic perceptions and behaviour, and further, that he understood intelligence services and intelligence relations to be an important part of the larger diplomatic relationship.

The message is long and substantive. It was important in the high-level topics it addressed, and by the fact that it was conveyed through covert channels; a secret message passed to French leaders through their clandestine services in London. So what did Menzies actually convey? Perhaps unsurprisingly, the intelligence chief began with intelligence news: the state of intelligence liaison between the Anglo-Americans and the Soviets. In short, the intelligence relationship with the Russians was bad, and it is clear that this, for Menzies, damaged overall trust and contributed to fears of Soviet intentions: despite Western requests 'for collaboration with the Russian special services, these give them practically nothing'. In contrast to the official stance of His Majesty's Government and the Supreme Headquarters Allied Expeditionary Force (SHAEF), the Western Allies were 'in no way kept informed of Russian intentions or as to their means of carrying on operations'.[27]

The fate of Germany was critical not just to postwar international diplomacy, but for postwar intelligence relations. For Menzies the two were linked, especially when one considered the intelligence prizes to be won from capturing and interrogating German intelligence officers. Yet poor intelligence relations contributed to his apprehension of Soviet intentions. 'Menzies greatly fears that the Russians will pursue a policy of a *fait accompli* in Germany', refusing to accept Allied control commissions in Berlin or anywhere else they occupied first.[28] He was 'very pessimistic'. As Germany was occupied, he feared Soviet counterespionage units would refuse to work with the Allies, and as a result all the criminals or agents of the German intelligence services, in which the Allies were interested, would take refuge in the Russian occupation zone. Menzies thought this might 'bring complete disaster in Germany'.

As the cable continues, we see even more clearly the potential of intelligence co-operation to affect the top levels of international diplomacy. Faced with Russian intransigence in Germany, Menzies promised to work closely with the French, even on the subject of a French occupation zone – a core issue of French diplomacy and strategy. Menzies promised to 'defend with the utmost energy the project of the idea of a French occupation zone: he considers it indispensable and considers that this zone will be the one with the best yield'.

What yield is he talking about?

Menzies was referring to the counterintelligence gains to be had from getting hold of German intelligence officers and agents, and especially those that had worked against the Soviet Union. According to the French messenger, Menzies would be counting on the French to get information from captured assets. The head of SIS, the Special Intelligence Service, believed the interrogation methods used by the British, those of 'persuasion and sweetness, yielding results only at the end of several months', would not be suitable for this situation, a postwar Germany defined in part by competition with the Soviet Union. Instead, as the DGER officer relayed, Menzies was in favour of 'more energetic methods employing at least, I say at least, the threat of torture'. Apparently, Menzies had discussed the issue with the American general Walter Bedell Smith, Chief of Staff to Supreme Allied Commander General Dwight Eisenhower. Menzies said Bedell Smith would 'give him a free hand', but Menzies was relying 'mainly on the energy of the French to get quick results from important agents arrested'.

In summing up, the DGER officer underscored the importance of these revelations for intelligence relationships and for wider international diplomacy. He told Paris that Allied relations with the Soviets 'are not good and the English are pessimistic'. He felt that Menzies 'voluntarily gave me these confidences to show me that the Franco–Soviet Treaty [an alliance signed between France and the USSR less than two months before] has surprises for us and perhaps not the success we believe'. The officer felt it important to note that Menzies' effort to sway the French against the Soviets spanned the British intelligence services: 'with the exception of Dansey, all our British comrades are making similar appeals with the French contacts'. Again, this shows the weight these figures put on intelligence relations – and personal relationships – believing their appeals could shape not just French intelligence posture but France's diplomatic outlook. Menzies promised the French that he sought real intelligence co-operation with France 'because he will need us'. Meanwhile, the French officer urged his chiefs to see that the DGER made an effort to mount intelligence missions into Germany alongside the British.[29]

As a piece of archival evidence, this cable is incredible. It gives a remarkably intimate look into the views of leading British, French and American figures, many of whom were intelligence leaders handling a lot of intelligence. It exists today only because Menzies passed a secret verbal message to the French in Paris through the French secret services in London, a message which was then intercepted by GC&CS, the SIGINT agency under Menzies' control, before being preserved in their archives and then declassified around 70 years later. It shows clearly how intelligence relationships between sovereign states can have a direct impact on larger diplomatic relationships. Consider how the poor intelligence-sharing relationship with the Russians played such a role in Menzies' anxiety and apprehension about larger Soviet intentions going forward. Or how this proof point was used in an effort to warn French security services that the recent Franco–Soviet Treaty 'might not be the success' they believed.

Just as important, however, is the obvious centrality of personal relationships in larger, state-to-state intelligence relationships. Whether or not it is viewed from a place of cynicism, Menzies' effort to split the French and Russians was an incredibly bold and risky manoeuvre. 'C' addressed many of the most important and most sensitive issues of Allied strategy and international diplomacy: from the occupation of Germany and the role of torture in interrogations to come, all the way up to Big Three relations and fear of future Soviet intentions. Menzies took a risk by touching on such issues even in a verbal exchange. That he did so speaks in part to the urgency he felt in his objectives, but also the trust he felt towards his French counterparts. Consider the key emphases provided by the DGER officer: the cable was 'absolutely secret'; Menzies 'voluntarily gave me these confidences'; 'employing at least, I say at least, the threat of torture'; and 'all our British comrades are making the same appeal to their French contacts'. Setting the substance of the message aside, comments like these reveal an exceptional level of trust and belief in the power of personal relationships to affect strategic and political orientations.

International intelligence archives offer insight into the formation and maintenance of intelligence relationships, both between intelligence officers and sovereign states. The SRH of the American NSA help to underscore the role of circumstances and culture in forming and preserving these connections. British SIGINT files demonstrate not only the importance of personal relationships in state-to-state intelligence relations, but also the way clandestine intelligence liaison can have an impact on issues of high diplomacy and grand strategy – and how these issues are interconnected.

The role of circumstances, culture and personal relations are not static, but they are timeless. If we bring these insights forward to today, we can see some ways that contemporary intelligence relationships should be judged, and some questions that could shed light on intelligence liaison in international diplomacy. In the Ukraine war, for instance, observers have witnessed an incredible amount of Five Eyes intelligence being shared with a partner outside of that club.[30] In particular, recent reporting has underscored the significance of personal relations in the intelligence co-operation between Ukraine and the United States, and how these have helped sustain that relationship even during the darkest moments of this war.[31]

This research offers lenses through which contemporary intelligence relationships could be examined, at least in the future. It suggests that while much exists through which to understand the functioning of ongoing liaison, one must be cognisant that great humility is required, and that much of the detail and nuance remain out of reach, in inaccessible documents that may not ever be released to the public. Perhaps most of all, the intricacies of the personal relationships so central to clandestine work, and the trust that facilitates co-operation in this secret field, will remain hidden, possibly forever. Put simply, more documents and more accounts are going to be necessary to provide a clear sense of how intelligence relationships are functioning today, how personal relationships are contributing to the whole, and how clandestine co-operation is or is not shaping high policy and grand strategy.

Nevertheless, this research also makes clear that historians looking at contemporary intelligence issues between the West and Ukraine would do well to consider not just the material shared between partners or the institutional processes by which the relationship is built, nor just the way Western or Ukrainian national or professional cultures may have contributed to the working of the connection. Instead they must also look closely at the personal relationships between the key figures in the relationship to get a sense of the levels of trust that exist between them and how this lets the liaison function. Most of all, historians should be careful to consider how intelligence material or product may have shaped diplomatic and strategic decision-making, while also remaining open to the way in which intelligence liaison and personal relationships themselves may have contributed to international diplomacy.

1. On co-operation generally, see Michael Herman, *Intelligence Power in Peace and War*. Cambridge: Cambridge University Press, 1996, pp. 200–18; on the importance of GCHQ to British strategy, power and international standing after the Second World War, see John Ferris, *Behind the Enigma: the Authorized History of GCHQ, Britain's Secret Cyber-Intelligence Agency*. London: Bloomsbury, 2020, in particular pp. 267–8; see also Intelligence and Security Committee of Parliament, International partnerships, Chairman: The Rt Hon. Sir Julian Lewis, MP, presented to Parliament pursuant to sections 3 of the Justice and Security Act 2013, London: HH Associates Ltd. on behalf of the Controller of His Majesty's Stationery Office, 2023, pp. 1–3, https:isc.independent.gov.uk/.

2. Brett M Holmgren, Assistant Secretary, Bureau of Intelligence and Research, US Department of State. Intelligence and diplomacy: a new model for a new era. Remarks, Cipher Brief Annual Threat Conference, Sea Island, Georgia, 8 October 2023, https:www.state.gov/intelligence-and-diplomacy-a-new-model-for-a-new-era/; Iain Thomson. CISA boss says US alliance with Ukraine over past year is closer than Five Eyes. *The Register*, 10 August 2023, https:www.theregister.com/2023/08/10/cisa_ukraine_black_hat/; Associated Press. US diplomat says intelligence from 'Five Eyes' nations helped Canada to link India to Sikh's killing, 24 September 2023, https:apnews.com/article/canada-us-india-sikh-activist-killing-intelligence-c475ac129e09e5f1c9ebf68eaaf247ab. See also, in this collection, Gill Bennett, Intelligence, communication and leaks: the perennial paradox of secret information.

3. Natasha Bertrand, Jim Sciutto and Kylie Atwood. CIA director dispatched to Moscow to warn Russia over troop buildup near Ukraine. CNN, 5 November 2021, https:edition.cnn.com/2021/11/05/politics/bill-burns-moscow-ukraine/index.html; Olivia Gazis and Margaret Brennan. CIA Director William Burns to travel to Cairo for further hostage talks. CBS News, 9 February 2024, https:www.cbsnews.com/news/hamas-israel-hostage-talks-cia-director-william-burns-cairo/; Jonathan Broder. Back door diplomats: CIA chiefs on secret missions. *Spytalk*, 4 February 2024, https:www.spytalk.co/p/back-door-diplomats-cia-chiefs-on.

4. Richard J Aldrich (ed.). *British Intelligence, Strategy and the Cold War, 1945–51*. New York: Routledge, 1993, pp. 1–3. The UK is frank around the destruction or the retention of many documents pertaining to the secret services: National Archives. How to look for records of…intelligence and security services, https:www.nationalarchives.gov.uk/help-with-your-research/research-guides/intelligence-and-security-services/.

5. Shane Harris. The time US spies thought Al Qaeda was ready to nuke DC. *The Daily Beast*, 10 September 2016, https:www.thedailybeast.com/the-time-us-spies-thought-al-qaeda-was-ready-to-nuke-dc; see Hayden reference the episode in his Foreword in Michael Smith, *The Real Special Relationship: the True Story of How MI6 and the CIA Work Together*. New York: Arcade Publishing, 2022, pp. 14–16.

6.   Ferris, *Behind the Enigma*, pp. 268, 313, 714.

7.   On trust, see the comments made by Michael Hayden, former NSA director and former CIA director, in Foreword and Sir John Scarlett, former chief of the Secret Intelligence Service (MI6), Introduction, in Smith, *Relationship*, pp. 14–29; see also comments by John Ferris included in Nico Hines, Why the NSA told Henry Kissinger to drop dead when he tried to cut intel links with Britain.
     The Daily Beast, 23 October 2020, https:www.thedailybeast.com/why-the-nsa-told-henry-kissinger-to-drop-dead-when-he-tried-to-cut-intel-links-with-britain.

8.   See in this collection Calder Walton, Declassifying intelligence about Ukraine: an applied history analysis; see also Huw Dylan and Thomas J Maguire, Secret intelligence and public diplomacy in the Ukraine war. *Survival,* vol 64, no 4, 2022, pp. 33–74.

9.   See Neveen Shaaban Abdalla, Philip H J Davies, Kristian Gustafson, Dan Lomas and Steven Wagner. Intelligence and the war in Ukraine: part 2. *War on the Rocks*, 19 May 2022, https:warontherocks.com/2022/05/intelligence-and-the-war-in-ukraine-part-2/; Press briefing by Press Secretary Jen Psaki, 3 March 2022. The White House, https:www.whitehouse.gov/briefing-room/press-briefings/2022/03/03/press-briefing-by-press-secretary-jen-psaki-march-3rd-2022/.

10. Abdalla, Davies, Gustafson, Lomas and Wagner, Ukraine: part 2.

11. Adam Entous and Michael Schwirtz. The spy war: how the CIA secretly helps Ukraine fight Putin. *New York Times*, 25 February 2024, https:www.nytimes.com/2024/02/25/world/europe/cia-ukraine-intelligence-russia-war.html#:~:text=The%20C.I.A.%20and%20other%20American,is%20Ukraine%20the%20only%20beneficiary.

12. Ferris, *Behind the Enigma,* pp. 163–222; Richard J Aldrich. *GCHQ: the Uncensored Story of Britain's Most Secret Intelligence Agency.* London: Harper Press, 2010, pp. 18–25.

13. Ferris, *Behind the Enigma*, pp. 213–16.

14. See Martin Thomas, Signals intelligence and Vichy France, 1940–44: intelligence in defeat. *Intelligence and National Security*, vol 14, no 1, 1999, pp. 176–200; Hugues Canuel, French aspirations and Anglo-Saxon suspicions: France, signals intelligence and the UK–USA agreement at the dawn of the Cold War. *Journal of Intelligence History*, vol 12, no 1, 2013, pp. 76–92; Roger Faligot, France, Sigint and the Cold War. *Intelligence and National Security,* vol 16, no 1, 2001, pp. 177–208.

15. Douglas Porch. *The French Secret Services: from the Dreyfus Affair to the Gulf War.* Oxford: Oxford University Press, 1997.

16. See for instance National Archives HW/74/1/S.S.0015 and HW/74/2/S.S.0313.

17. Ferris, *Behind the Enigma*, pp. 330–4.

18. National Archives and Records Administration. RG457/9002/24, SRH-107. Problems of the Special Security System in World War II, pp. 6–9. [NND947022].

19. Ibid, pp. 36–8.

20. Ibid.

21. National Archive and Records Administration. RG457/9002/24, SRH-110, Operations of the MIS War Department, London, Special Security Operations European Theater, pp. 1–3. [NND947022].
22. National Archives. FO/1093/235, Menzies to Loxley, 9 May 1942.
23. François Kersaudy. *Churchill and de Gaulle.* London: Fontana Press, 1990, pp. 305–15.
24. National Archives. HW/74/2/S.S.0547, 31 December 1943.
25. Ibid.
26. National Archives. HW74/14/S.S.4322, 'NOCQ to Soustelle, Passy and Manuel', 20 April 1945.
27. Ibid.
28. Ibid.
29. Ibid.
30. Abdalla, Davies, Gustafson, Lomas and Wagner, Ukraine: Part 2.
31. Entous and Schwirtz, The spy war.

INTELLIGENCE
AND CONTEMPORARY
CONFLICT

Soviet army soldiers in an armoured vehicle
during a patrol in Kabul, Afghanistan, 1988.

'SHOULD I STAY OR SHOULD I GO?': THE UNITED STATES, NATO, INTELLIGENCE AND THE WAR IN AFGHANISTAN, 2001–22

John Ferris

Few countries are easier to invade than Afghanistan, with its economy poor, its population divided and its armies weak. Few countries are harder to control. Far from being the graveyard of empires, Afghanistan mostly has been their playground. If Afghanis defeated foreign occupiers, outsiders routinely manipulated its politics and stole its land.[1] This paper will assess modern invasions of Afghanistan and ask: why do foreign states invade it? How far do their leaders understand what they are doing? How do ideology and perception affect these ideas? Why is occupation so difficult? Why do occupiers leave? How does intelligence affect these outcomes?

Twice, between 1838 and 1842 and again from 1878 to 1881, Britain sought to occupy Afghanistan, because decision-makers thought the task would be easy and was necessary to prevent foreign attacks on and subversion against India. Britain invaded Afghanistan from habit. Expansionist forces within its Indian administration drove its empire there. Danger always stood beyond its borders – or things could be made to look that way. War, better than peace, suited frontier officials seeking promotion. Indian authorities invaded Afghanistan because they thought it could be easily made a protectorate and used to dominate Central Asia. They were misinformed; this invasion stemmed from intelligence failure, and optimistic and confused policy. Indian authorities also feared that Afghanistan might work with Russia and inspire plots against their rule, especially by Muslims.[2] The first invasion failed disastrously, and the second effort was little more successful. Then Britain adopted a new strategy towards Afghanistan, which produced acceptable military costs and political results: not to invade the country, but rather to forge decent relations with its monarch and subsidise him so he would not threaten India, while annexing parts of its territory.

Soviet leaders understood the potential risks of invading Afghanistan, but still did so between 1978 and 1986, for reasons similar to those which had inspired British invasions: because they thought occupation would be easy and was necessary to prevent threats to the USSR. The Soviets did this by unleashing Islamic insurgency against the country while enabling the United States to build a bastion on the edge of Soviet power, a possibility which Soviet intelligence grossly overstated.[3] In the 1990s, after the USSR abandoned this policy, Pakistan worked with some Afghans to control Afghanistan and make it an ally.[4]

Between 1989 and 2001, a new regime emerged in Afghanistan. The Taliban was a Salafi jihadist movement affiliated with another one, al-Qaeda, which was based in Afghanistan. Under Osama bin Laden, al-Qaeda attacked American forces in the Middle East. Slowly and reluctantly, the Clinton administration began military operations against al-Qaeda in Afghanistan, as the Bush administration was preparing to do by August 2001. Neither administration wished to invade Afghanistan or fight the Taliban.[5] However, 9/11, the greatest intelligence failure ever linked to Afghanistan, forced the US to attack out of self-defence, because al-Qaeda was based in that country. Other Western countries followed suit, putting NATO multilateralism and old school ties into action to show the wounded hyperpower it still had friends.

The Taliban withered against the combination of its Afghan enemies, Special Operations Forces (SOF) from the 'Five Eyes' and American air power, but its real weakness was political. Taliban rule was opposed by all non-Pashtuns, and supported (in contrast to 'tolerated') by few Pashtuns: half the population aided its defeat, while the rest refused it much help. When Taliban weakness became apparent, the opportunists in its forces (most of the native Afghanis) switched sides, which was how they had joined in the first place. The Taliban regime shattered, and its remnants fled into Pakistan.[6] Western states attempted to replace the Taliban by creating a good government, which became the Islamic Republic of Afghanistan, and loaning thousands of NATO soldiers to establish its rule across the country. This was an honest aim but not an easy one, nor were the liberal democracies of NATO the first states to think they could make Afghanistan a better place. In 1838 and 1878, Britons believed they would do so, as did the Soviets in 1979. In 2002 Western states gave a decent but militarily weak Afghan politician, Hamid Karzai, power in Afghanistan, and encouraged his efforts to create a national following and legitimacy. This task had some initial success, because Western forces were strong and Afghanis were weary of war, while Karzai and his backers were pragmatic enough to buy many local military leaders – or warlords – into the process. Knowledgeable commentators like Ahmed Rashid criticised this strategy, but it was hard to avoid.[7] Yet NATO's military and political policies were decoupled and its armies conducted irregular operations in a civil war against many enemies, including Taliban forces, which tried to regain the territory they used to control.

This victory was too good to be true. American leaders had not wanted this war, had attacked Afghanistan out of necessity and had no idea what victory meant. In 2001–2, the only victory which the American people would have recognised was Osama's scalp, which might have reduced the pressure on Washington to stay in Afghanistan. Instead, the inability to destroy al-Qaeda pinned the US and NATO to Afghanistan. In hindsight, the only feasible way to win this war was for NATO to use this astonishing victory not to impose a government of its own choosing but instead to convince Afghans not to attack the West again. Simply withdrawing after the Taliban was smashed, but pledging to return whenever necessary, might have sufficed. The Taliban understood how badly they had been whipped and how reckless their policy of sheltering al-Qaeda and its attacks on Western targets had been. Instead, because the US had invaded Afghanistan for defensive purposes and won such a stunning victory without winning a general war on terror, its leaders imagined that they could ignore history. But history bit back. American leaders misconstrued the causes for their victory, which really occurred because Taliban forces fought their version of conventional war, exposing themselves to a deadly combination of local and foreign enemies. Once the Taliban reverted to irregular warfare, this vulnerability declined. Moreover, Americans did not appreciate the difference between success in invading a country and success in occupying it, which also deformed their policy regarding Iraq. American leaders took these events as proof that the so-called 'revolution in military affairs' was working as planned, and would do so again: this false reading was extrapolated to US military planning against Iraq, which it polluted. Meanwhile, NATO forces began 20 years of involvement in Afghanistan. They started without a strategy, backing a government which controlled just Kabul, Kandahar and a few other cities while relying on warlord militias to run some places and using SOF to engage Taliban forces on the Afghani–Pakistan border. No one controlled the countryside, but the Taliban and other groups also opposed to NATO slowly re-emerged.

The United States then carried the polluted strategy from Iraq back to Afghanistan. During 2006–7, American forces temporarily overcame military failure in Iraq. They did so primarily through politics, by using their dominant (almost colonial) position to work with some Shiite and Sunni leaders in Iraq, and, applying those alliances and innovative tactics, to defeat their common foes.[8] Americans conceptualised this success as stemming from a liberal form of counterinsurgency, which they made into a doctrine and exported to Afghanistan. Meanwhile, during the 2008 presidential election, to demonstrate that he was reliable on matters of national security, Barack Obama announced his intention to win the war in Afghanistan. President Obama's politics and American military doctrine drove the US to a more aggressive strategy across all of Afghanistan. Americans did not realise they had succeeded in Iraq only because levers could be pulled there which did not exist in Afghanistan, like an effective state and political movements able to unify much of the population. Even worse, the US announced a ludicrous strategy which would surge forces to Afghanistan for 18 months, solve every problem immediately and then return to previous force levels. This statement notified the Taliban that if they were not crushed in this 18-month period, their enemy would weaken.

The American concept of counterinsurgency meant the allocation of Western forces in large numbers for long periods of time to defeat guerrillas and pacify one area after another until a stable national government emerged.[9] No previous foreign occupier of Afghanistan conducted anything like that form of counterinsurgency, as against what might be loosely called 'hybrid', 'irregular', 'asymmetric' or 'unconventional' warfare, which imperial British thinkers conceptualised through terms like 'small wars' or 'imperial policing'.[10] All prior conquerors of Afghanistan used politics and bribes to win support (or tolerance) in the country, but nothing like counterinsurgency. During 1556–1707, the Mughal Empire controlled much of Afghanistan, through garrisons in Kabul and Kandahar, subsidies to Pashtun leaders, and frequently the despatch of large conventional armies to defeat rebels. This policy was expensive, and after mixed success for a century it collapsed. The Mughals faced increasing problems across India, concluded that expenditure on Afghanistan was a low priority, cut it and thus lost the country.[11] The British lacked the force even to attempt counterinsurgency in Afghanistan, where they merely occupied Kabul and Kandahar and ruled the country-side through the tiniest presence and lowest cost possible. Between 1838 and 1841, for example, British forces garrisoned the cities, while political officers maintained influence in rural areas through bribes and paid levies. For two years, occupation faced little opposition. Afghanis were willing to let Britain intervene in dynastic politics, but not to take them over. As Britain began to do that, opposition rose. Financial problems in India caused Britain to cut its subsidies in Afghanistan, which undercut its ability to maintain alliances. Resentment at the presence of foreign occupiers, and the havoc it raised on the Afghani economy, caused unrest, which in turn created uprisings.[12]

After 1881, driven by experience, the ability to learn from history and the desire to solve the Afghani problem at the lowest possible cost, Britain created a new and effective policy towards Afghanistan, which lasted until 1947 and the end of the Raj.[13] Britain abandoned any effort to occupy Afghanistan, though for precisely that reason it had to conduct counterinsurgency along the North-West Frontier. Britain annexed the southernmost areas of Afghanistan, defined by the Durand Line, which survive as the 'tribal areas' of Pakistan. Britain disciplined Baluchi and Pashtun tribes through diplomacy, raids and subsidies, using force only as a tool to convince tribespeople that they should accept bribes not to bother the British. Britain created forces, like the Khyber Rifles, essentially to pay Pashtuns to be soldiers rather than bandits. It pursued negative and limited aims through minimal presence, sought never to challenge customs or religion, tried to find local allies and tried to minimise casualties among civilians. When air power joined the arsenal, Britain executed a policy of zero collateral damage among civilians, and airstrikes killed few if any civilians on the North-West Frontier.[14] Seventy years later, NATO was less scrupulous. Britain found operations in these areas hard, because the population, including well-armed veterans of the Indian army, played its hand well against Britain. As the tribal areas were hard to control, this approach was wise – but not cheap. They became a hotbed of Pashtun resistance and Muslim challenges to the British Empire, while their population maintained close links with their cousins across the border. They rebelled when Afghanistan declared war on Britain in 1919, posing a major problem which Britain still contained. Nonetheless, this policy kept Britain from strategic quicksand and made Afghanistan a buffer which Britain could defend against Russia or not, as it chose. Until 1947 that helped keep Britain and Russia from war, despite constant rivalry and occasional hostility between the two countries.

The USSR had a sophisticated model of counterinsurgency, originally developed from fighting another group of Islamic guerrillas, the *Basmachi*, in Central Asia. It aimed to turn struggles for national liberation into class wars by combining ruthless attacks on guerrillas and their friends with efforts to split local societies and bribe support into existence by redistributing land from richer to poorer peasants; and by using amnesties to weaponise some guerrillas while isolating the intransigent. This approach, associated more with the KGB, the Soviet foreign intelligence and domestic security service, than the army, beat serious guerrillas with strong support in Central Asia, Lithuania and Ukraine, partly because the Red Army destroyed conventional enemy forces and bases across borders.[15] At the start of the occupation of Afghanistan, the Politburo and KGB envisioned something similar, 'a gradual attack on the position of the tribal reaction, the showing of flexibility and a differentiated approach to various tribes and socio-economic strata', splitting 'moderate Moslem leaders' from 'reactionary clerical circles' and convincing 'the leaders and elders of the most warlike tribes' to stop fighting. Soviet leaders advocated a radical redistribution of land to build rural allies and arm them – unsuccessfully. As landholding patterns in Afghanistan were generally equitable and accepted, while efforts at reform were violent and incompetent, these measures created far fewer friends than enemies. Eighteen months after the invasion, local commanders warned that this failure was crippling 'the class division among the peasantry and the enlistment of its broad masses to the side of popular democratic rule'. The KGB pursued other parts of its classic counterinsurgency programme more successfully. It had some political success with Pashtun tribes in Afghanistan, and even more across the Durand Line, hampering support for the Mujahideen and their supply lines. To pressure that regime, it organised terrorist bombings which killed hundreds of civilians in Pakistan. It manipulated divisions within the Mujahideen to make some of them defect and become militia, armed by the government. Contrary to usual Soviet practice, however, these forces were allies, not puppets, doubly so after the Red Army left Afghanistan, and thus a mixed blessing. In 1992 the decision of these militias to abandon the regime destroyed it. Precisely the same thing happened in Afghanistan between 2016 and 2022.[16]

The USSR could not apply its model of counterinsurgency in Afghanistan, because it never had enough forces or control over the population. Ironically, this lack of force drove Moscow to rely even more heavily on it. Like its American counterpart in Vietnam, the Soviet army did not wish to conduct counterinsurgency, which it left to the KGB, but to follow its book for war in Europe.[17] That focused on complex fire procedures and fast-moving mechanised forces. The army fought as large units and formations, using (as a contemporary CIA analysis said) 'stereotyped search and destroy operations'. Battalions tried to trap small groups of Mujahideen through slow-moving assaults, while divisions were deployed down valleys in stately echelons. Usually, Soviet security was too weak to achieve surprise, its reconnaissance could not find the enemy, its forces were too few to trap and kill guerrillas, or efforts at combined arms and fancy plans turned into bloody clashes between light infantry. Constant attacks were launched to take pieces of ground, which were abandoned, reoccupied, left and counterattacked again. Both unintentionally and to deter peasants from supporting guerrillas, Soviet firepower killed hundreds of thousands of civilians and drove millions into exile.[18]

The fundamental problem for occupiers of Afghanistan was the inability to coordinate political and military matters, which is essential for any form of counterinsurgency. The great Afghani opponent of the Soviet invasion, Ahmed Shah Masoud, told his officers:

> The strategy of the Mujahideen is a long-term strategy. All the Mujahideen can do is harass the enemy, make them tired and their lives difficult and dangerous…We must prolong the war so the cost of the war will finally bleed the enemy to death. The cost will be economic, in manpower and equipment, and the end will come through crisis and the loss of public and political support. The enemy cannot smash the Mujahideen, the vanguard of the people, as this is a national resistance and a holy war. In the end, we will not *defeat* the enemy. We will force them to *retreat*.[19]

This statement reflected Masoud's particular grasp of guerrilla warfare, applied to a Salafi jihadist strategy, but since 1838 other Afghani leaders have followed similar ideas when occupied, and to good effect.

As Alexander Burnes, Britain's chief political officer in Kabul, wrote in 1841, 'More fighting still! when will this country be pacified?'[20] In 1986, Sergei Akhromeyev, Soviet deputy minister of defence, wrote:

> There is no single piece of land in this country which has not been occupied by a Soviet soldier. Nevertheless, the majority of the territory remains in the hands of rebels...There is no single military problem that has arisen and that has not been solved, and yet there is still no result. The whole problem is in the fact that military results are not followed up by political.[21]

Commentators routinely assess this situation by reference to history, usually by retelling legends of 'The Afghans: a people often oppressed and tormented, but ultimately invincible!' variety.[22] Yet historical patterns are there to be seen. Afghanistan was saved because Afghanis could make occupation expensive, while no outsider wanted to pay much to control it. During 1845, right after it abandoned Afghanistan, Britain crushed a greater power, the Sikh kingdom, because it mattered. Afghanistan did not. Except in 1979, when occupied, most Afghanis were neither collaborators nor resistors but opportunists who acted rationally in response to their perception of power. Revolts came out of the blue whenever an occupier's weakness convinced opportunists they were safe to move and able to profit from it. Between 1838 and 2001, every invasion of Afghanistan destroyed the incumbent regime but failed to keep its successor in power. Stable governments emerged only a decade after invaders withdrew, through ruthless conquest. Afghanistan is easy to invade and hard to conquer, because the country is fragmented, its state is weak and Afghanis want to be there more than any invaders do. Britain and the USSR were beaten not because their armies were crushed, but when they realised victory would cost more than they wanted to pay. Afghanis defeat invaders by raising the bar for victory, and not even to a high level, because attackers have little will for the job. Foreign occupiers leave and lose because, after initial enthusiasm, their will and allocation of resources slowly erode until a tipping point emerges. The only way foreign states can dominate Afghanistan is by finding a local ally which wants to co-operate with them and is able to manage the country while being aided on the cheap.

Afghanis have beaten England, the USSR and the United States once each, and have drawn with Britain twice; not a bad record for a small

Osama bin Laden sits with his son Mohammed
and a senior aide, Kandahar, Afghanistan, 2001.

power against such great ones. Yet Britain, Russia, Iran and Pakistan also found it easy to annex much of Afghanistan and to manipulate its politics. Afghanis are unusually willing – aye, eager – to let outside powers interfere in their politics, especially during civil strife. Afghanistan is simple to dominate from outside. Positive and ambitious aims are hard to achieve there, but limited and negative ones are easy, such as stopping it from being a problem. In Afghanistan, one can get much for little – with the right ally. Its weakness is the same as its strength: fragmentation, isolation and poverty. The Afghan state has always depended on outside aid to control its population and territory. A tiny subsidy kept it from bothering the Raj at key points, as in 1916. In 1857, a subsidy of £220,000 helped keep Afghanistan out of the Indian 'mutiny', when British authorities thought it could take Punjab, with devastating consequences for the Raj. From 1950 to 1978, foreign aid provided 40% of Afghanistan's budget, and even more for both sides between 1979 and 1990; the Taliban conquered the country largely through the aid of a few million dollars and a few thousand *ghazis* from Pakistan.[23] Afghanis are easy to buy; far easier than they are to fight. The trick is to avoid trying to conquer the country, while finding an Afghani who will keep it out of your hair. Alas, NATO could find no such figure after Masoud's murder by al-Qaeda on 10 September 2001.

Compared to historical norms, the case of Western counterinsurgency in Afghanistan during 2001–22 was unusual in two ways. Britain and the USSR never invaded Afghanistan for its own sake, but always because of its links, imagined or real, to broader issues, distant dangers and internal/external threats. The value of Afghanistan has been easy to exaggerate. Intelligence failures, confusion and optimism colour the policy of invaders of Afghanistan. These problems were true between 2001 and 2022, yet still Western countries were there only after having been attacked. They may have been paranoid, but they had real enemies, and reasons for fear. During the 1990s, they ignored Afghanistan and received al-Qaeda. Even more unusual, throughout NATO's presence in Afghanistan, was the low level of armed opposition it encountered. This unprecedented event happened because NATO was not trying to conquer the country but rather was intervening in a civil war, where it had friends alongside enemies and offered aid at a scale beyond the avarice even of Afghanis. Moreover, intelligence and unmanned aerial vehicles (UAVs) reduced collateral damage among civilians, which angered Afghanis. NATO was, however, fighting among (and to some degree against) Pashtuns, with their traditions of jihad and resistance to occupation or to the presence of any outsiders, whether in Kabul or just across the valley. Though most Pashtuns remained quiescent, NATO faced several opponents: people irritated at any foreign presence or the state; opium smugglers; and the Taliban, which drew some support from Pashtuns on either side of the Durand Line and, as ever, used foreigners to substitute for a lack of assistance from Afghanis.

NATO was fighting a guerrilla war. Historically, most insurgencies fail; poor counterinsurgents crush bad guerrillas, but good ones are hard to beat. Only dirty means can defeat tough and ruthless insurgents. Nice intentions backfire. Ambition is dangerous. The fundamental tenets of liberal counterinsurgency – the pursuit of good and effective government – can create more enemies than friends, because to extend the reach of an unpopular state strengthens rather than weakens resistance to it, while to give aid increases corruption.[24] In counterinsurgency, politics matters more than force, and the two must be coordinated. Failure in these areas was NATO's greatest problem, as it had been for Britain and the USSR. Again, NATO could not win this war; only its Afghan ally could do so. Nor could this war be won by force alone – politics was necessary. NATO forces had to be strong enough to block a Taliban resurgence, and show that the Islamic Republic of Afghanistan was here to stay; but in doing so Western policy created enemies by their presence, the casualties they inflicted on civilians, and by their attempts to force an unpopular government (or any government at all) on Pashtuns and to attack part of the local economy, the opium trade. If NATO's actions ever created an alliance between its armed opponents and large numbers of Pashtuns, it would lose. They wanted to be in Afghanistan more than Westerners did. Westerners lacked the ruthlessness and vested interest needed to conquer them.

NATO's sole reasons to be there were self-interest and self-defence: to maintain a government able to keep Afghanistan from threatening the West. Such a government might take many forms, but it could never be one we would like. New aims emerged after the invasion, like nation-building and social reform, which were tertiary in strategic significance but important to the willingness of Western populations to support the war. These matters also confused Western sensibilities regarding what interests were at stake. Liberal democracy or women's rights, alas, could not be imposed by the bayonet. NATO could not rule Afghanistan as a colony or through a puppet, but any other kind of regime would disappoint us. NATO could achieve limited and negative aims, although they might with dangerous ease become positive, ambitious and impossible. Among NATO countries, public support for the mission was too weak to sustain a long case of stalemate. In counterinsurgency, especially among Pashtuns, as in judo, what you do matters no more than what you do not do. The key considerations were: how far can one pacify Afghanistan? How far can one make a state effective? Afghanistan never has been pacified, nor has the state ever controlled the village. NATO strategy could work only if it did not ask too high a price of Westerners, or of Afghanis. Alas, that is precisely what happened.

Strong command and control, and the unification of military and political efforts, are necessary for any effective campaign against guerrillas. These matters were remarkably confused during NATO's campaign in Afghanistan. As during prior British and Soviet occupations, NATO worked with national Afghani leaders who disliked their external allies and their own reliance on foreigners, and followed different policies, often contradictory. NATO leaders increasingly mistrusted those of the Islamic Republic of Afghanistan. The latter failed to create a national political framework or state; its credibility among the population eroded, while its military declined in quality as it rose in quantity. That government relied on local militias to survive, but they were free to defect at will. The Western presence was so large as to damage the economy; massive numbers of civilians moved to the cities, while aid encouraged corruption across the country. Every province of Afghanistan was garrisoned by a different NATO member, their actions allegedly coordinated at a national level. This coordination failed, amidst a huge and ineffective command in Kabul. Every NATO member had different rules of engagement for combat, which many of them avoided, and all eyed the exits. The real lever for decision-making was an alliance of the willing under American leadership, meaning that the Five Eyes contingents co-operated fairly closely, much less so even with the most warlike of other NATO members. Intelligence was collected and processed in silos, the largest of them being the Five Eyes, and not shared across the command. NATO forces were ludicrously small. In 2007–9, 1,000 Canadian soldiers were NATO's sole force in Helmand and Kandahar provinces, areas which could not be controlled even when reinforced by 30,000 American and 2,000 British soldiers. All of these forces vanished from combat around 2011, and some were deformed by the process. Elements within the American, Australian and British SOF fighting the campaign became death squads, exploiting their chance to kill for fun. Pacification failed at national and provincial levels. The enemy could not be destroyed, because it was hard to find. The Taliban re-established its presence across much Pashtun territory.

Against these failures, in technical terms, the Western campaign of counterinsurgency across Western and Central Asia took forms never seen before, with remarkable effect in certain ways, particularly for intelligence and strike. Imagery and the interception of mobile phone communication routinely provided real-time intelligence which guided immediate, precise and distant strikes by SOF and UAVs, or drones, against enemies who could never block and could not easily evade these attacks. By historical standards, this combination enabled counterinsurgents to kill an unusually large number of hostile forces and leaders with few shots wasted, and for small amounts of collateral damage. This combination enabled a strategy of mowing the lawn, of simply containing a problem without solving it, which is no mean feat when fighting guerrillas or irregulars. Still, thousands of innocents were slain. The enemy sometimes controlled human sources trusted by NATO intelligence services, and hijacked NATO forces to serve their own purpose. In practical terms, this combination of intelligence and precision enabled NATO to continue an effective campaign of counterinsurgency after ground forces surged away and also contained the rage which consumed Afghanis when their civilians were slaughtered. Unfortunately, this outcome merely sustained a stalemate. It did not fuel victory, and the infrastructure and subsidies required to maintain this strategy were enormously costly.[25]

Few if any civilian experts on Afghanistan believed this campaign could succeed, and the officers commanding the effort never thought they were winning. The war in Afghanistan seemed increasingly pointless and endless, expensive and unwinnable. The death of Osama bin Laden psychologically detached Westerners from support for the war, as did a decline in fear of Salafi jihadist terrorism. The campaign was increasingly characterised by inertia, and the question became 'Should I stay or should I go?' By 2020, the two candidates in the United States presidential

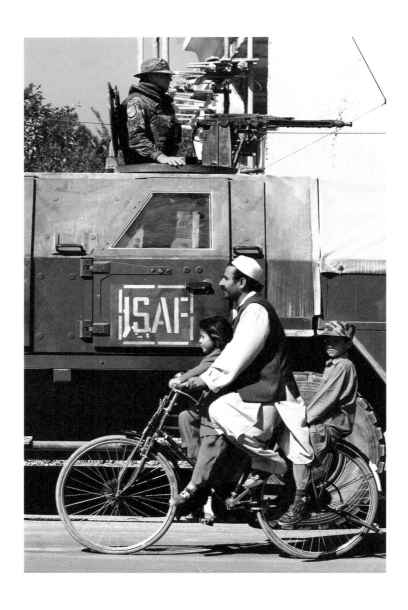

An Afghani family rides past a
German International Security Assistance
Force soldier manning an armoured personnel
carrier in Kabul, Afghanistan, 2002.

election both wished to abandon Afghanistan. Had he won, Donald Trump would probably have acted as Joe Biden did, though perhaps more competently. Biden, taking a page from the Richard Nixon play-book, chose to abandon Afghanistan by pursuing a decent time interval between the moment the United States left and the moment the regime collapsed.[26] His expectations proved wildly over-optimistic, yet another failure by foreigners to predict Afghani behaviour. Confronted with a choice between fighting the Taliban for a few years and then losing, the regime simply collapsed, precisely as South Vietnam had done in 1974, with soldiers and militias surrendering, politicians fleeing, civilians lost in fear and confusion.[27]

The process of wars in Afghanistan, Iraq and Vietnam have much in common, because all were driven by similar characteristics within American decision-making. In each case, extraordinarily complicated systems of decision-making, managerial and technocratic approaches, and faith in American exceptionalism from historical patterns drove boom and bust strategies. Imperial British decision-makers had great patience for time, but little for cost. They could sustain long stalemates, as long as they could cap the cost, but rejected lengthy and expensive campaigns with no returns. They spent a century mowing the lawn on the North-West Frontier because it was cheap and unavoidable. However much stereotyping distorted their analysis of peoples, Britons had a shrewd sense of individual foreigners with whom they interacted, and with experience, often bitter, quickly recognised facts on the ground. Britain was too cost-conscious to have tolerated for long the expensive and profitless campaign conducted across Afghanistan by NATO between 2001 and 2022. Britain was rarely too strong for its own good, that classic problem of the United States. American leaders, conversely, have amazing tolerance for cost, but much less for time. They are willing to apply enormous resources to tertiary interests, and while they are slow to recognise failure, they then abruptly end a policy, which triggers the failure of the original political aim.

An alloy of ignorance and optimism, which information and intelligence could not scratch, underlay the policies of great powers confronting Afghanistan from 1830 to the present day. All of them suffered failure in net assessment, comparing the will and power of Afghanis to their own. This phenomenon illustrates how unexamined assumptions shape strategy and the interpretation of intelligence. These assumptions are related to the human tendency to simplify and stereotype when analysing complex and shifting matters. They took many forms: imperial anthropology, racism, orientalism, Whig paternalism, concepts of national character, and a model of the evolutionary modernisation of all peoples on Western lines, including movement towards matters like secularism, nationalism, communism and liberalism. The dominant idea was not drawn from the usual candidates, orientalism and racism, but from a kind of ethnocentrism, the assumption that one's own way of understanding and preferences for action are not just particular solutions to one's own special problems but rather the universal means of comprehension and action for all difficulties. Ethnocentrism affects every comparison between yourself and another, in this case the observation made by cultures which considered themselves to be leading the human evolution of another one which seemed far behind. During the 19th century, British views towards Afghanistan combined all the assumptions listed above, with imperial anthropology, liberalism and racism providing parallel explanations and predictions. Marxist–Leninist ethnocentrism drove Soviet policy. In the 1970s, Soviet leaders viewed Afghanistan through the prism of a universal doctrine preaching that all peoples passed through similar stages, facing problems with identical solutions. Soviet leaders thought their intervention in Afghanistan would have the same success as in Hungary in 1956 and Czechoslovakia in 1968. A great intelligence failure drove 9/11, alongside an assumption that American exceptionalism protected its territory from attack. Later Western policy in Afghanistan was driven by a peak sense of faith in the superiority of Western and liberal ideas. The failure of Western policy in Afghanistan eroded that sense of superiority and hubris.

1. The best single-volume history of Afghanistan is Thomas Barfield, *Afghanistan: a Cultural and Political History*. Princeton: Princeton University Press, 2010.
2. John Ferris. Lord Salisbury, secret intelligence and British policy toward Russia and Central Asia, 1874–1878, in John Robert Ferris, *Intelligence and Strategy: Selected Essays*. London: Routledge, 2005.
3. Cold War International History Project, Virtual Archive. *The Soviet Union and Afghanistan, 1978–1989: Documents from the Russian and East German Archives*, pp. 43, 58.
4. The essays in Scott Gates and Kaushik Roy (eds.), *War and State-Building in Afghanistan: Historical and Modern Perspectives*. London: Bloomsbury, 2015, especially Scott Gates, Kaushik Roy, Marianne Dahl and Håvard Mokliev Nygard, Continuity and change in asymmetric warfare in Afghanistan: from the Mughals to the Americans, pp. 21–42, offer excellent accounts of how foreign states handle or occupy Afghanistan; cf John Ferris, Invading Afghanistan, 1838–2006: politics and pacification, in John Ferris (ed.), *Canada in Kandahar: Calgary Papers in Military and Strategic Studies*, vol 1. Calgary: Centre for Military and Strategic Studies, 2007.
5. Steve Coll. *Ghost Wars: the Secret History of the CIA, Afghanistan and Bin Laden, from the Soviet Invasion to September 10, 2001*. New York: Penguin, 2004, pp. 189–576; Anonymous (Michael Scheuer). *Imperial Hubris: Why the West Is Losing the War on Terror*. Washington DC: Brassey's, 2004.
6. The best accounts of the campaign are Anthony H Cordesman, *The Lessons of Afghanistan: War Fighting, Intelligence, and Force Transformation*. Washington DC: Center for Strategic and International Studies, 2002; and Stephen Biddle, *Military Power: Explaining Victory and Defeat in Modern Battle*. Princeton: Princeton University Press, 2004.
7. Ahmed Rashid. *Descent into Chaos: the United States and the Failure of Nation Building in Pakistan, Afghanistan, and Central Asia*. New York: Viking, 2008, pp. 125–44, 171–240.
8. Celeste Ward Gventer, David Martin Jones and M L R Smith. *The New Counter-Insurgency Era in Critical Perspective*. London: Palgrave Macmillan, 2014; Thomas E Ricks. *The Gamble: General David Petraeus and the American Military Adventure in Iraq, 2006–2008*. London: Penguin, 2009.
9. US Army and US Marine Corps. Manual FM-3-24, 15.12.2006, Counterinsurgency, https:fas.org/irp/doddir/army/fm3-24fd.pdf.
10. David French. *The British Way in Counter-Insurgency, 1945–1967*. Oxford: Oxford University Press, 2011; John Ferris. Small wars and great games: the British Empire and hybrid warfare, 1700–1970, in Williamson Murray and Peter R Mansoor (eds.), *Hybrid Warfare: Fighting Complex Opponents from the Ancient World to the Present*. Cambridge: Cambridge University Press, 2012, pp. 199–224.
11. Kaushik Roy. Great Mughals, warfare and COIN in Afghanistan, 1520–1707, in Gates and Roy (eds.), *War and State-Building*, pp. 43–78.

12. Malcolm Yapp. *Strategies of British India: Britain, Iran and Afghanistan, 1798–1850*. Oxford: Clarendon Press, 1980, pp. 307–460; William Dalrymple. *Return of a King: the Battle for Afghanistan*. London: Bloomsbury, 2013.

13. John Ferris. Counter-insurgency and Empire: the British experience with Afghanistan and the North-West Frontier, 1838–1947, in Gates and Roy (eds.), *War and State-Building*, pp. 79–112.

14. Ibid, pp. 101–5.

15. Alexander Statiev. *The Soviet Counterinsurgency in the Western Borderlands*. Cambridge: Cambridge University Press, 2010.

16. Pavel K Baev. The conflict of war and politics in the Soviet intervention into Afghanistan, 1979–89, in Gates and Roy (eds.), *War and State-Building*, pp. 113–30; *Cold War International History Project Bulletin*, vols 8–9, 1996/7, pp. 16–35.

17. Lester W Grau. *The Bear Went Over the Mountain: Soviet Combat Tactics in Afghanistan*. London: Routledge, 1998; Lester W Grau and Michael I Gress (trans. and eds.). *The Soviet–Afghan War: How a Superpower Fought and Lost*. Lawrence: University Press of Kansas, 2002.

18. National Security Archive. *The September 11th Source Books, Volume II: Afghanistan: Lessons from the Last War*, The Soviet experience in Afghanistan: US analysis of the Soviet war in Afghanistan: declassified, John Prados (ed.), 9.10.01, Document Five, CIA, 1985, The Soviet invasion of Afghanistan: five years after; Mohammad Yousaf and Mark Adkin. *Afghanistan: the Bear Trap: the Defeat of a Superpower*. Barnsley: Casemate, 2001, p. 4; excerpt, 13.11.86, from Boris Gromov, Limited contingent, *Cold War International History Project*, Virtual Archive, Soviet Invasion of Afghanistan.

19. Will Davies and Abdullah Shariat. *Fighting Masoud's War*. South Melbourne: Lothian Books, 2004, p. 131.

20. Mohan Lal. *Life of the Amir Dost Mohammed Khan of Kabul*, vol 2. Oxford: Oxford University Press, 1978, p. 388; original Karachi, 1846.

21. *Cold War International History Project Bulletin*, vols 8–9, 1996/7, pp. 178–81.

22. Preface by Bert Georg Fragner in Christine Noelle, *State and Tribe in Nineteenth-Century Afghanistan: the Reign of Amir Dost Muhammad Khan (1926–1863)*. Abingdon: Routledge, 1997, p. ix.

23. Ferris, Invading Afghanistan.

24. D Michael Shafer. *Deadly Paradigms: the Failure of US Counterinsurgency Policy*. Princeton: Princeton University Press, 1988.

25. Special Inspector-General for Afghanistan Reconstruction. *What We Need to Learn: Lessons from Twenty Years of Afghanistan Reconstruction*. Arlington, VA, 2021. Excellent documentation of the counterinsurgency campaign in Afghanistan may be found in Seth Jones (ed.), *Counter-Insurgency in Afghanistan: RAND Counter Insurgency Study*, vol 4, RAND Corporation, 2008 and The Afghanistan Papers, *Washington Post*, 9–14 December 2019, https:www.washingtonpost.com/graphics/2019/investigations/afghanistan-papers/afghanistan-war-confidential-documents/#nav.

26. Jeffrey Kimball. *The Vietnam War Files: Uncovering the Secret History of Nixon-Era Strategy.* Lawrence: University Press of Kansas, 2004.
27. For Vietnam, cf Stephen T Hosmer, Konrad Kellen and Brian M Jenkins, *The Fall of South Vietnam: Statements by Vietnamese Military and Civilian Leaders.* New York: Crane Russak, 1980.

President Kennedy signs the arms embargo
against Cuba, October 1962.

DECLASSIFYING INTELLIGENCE ABOUT UKRAINE: AN APPLIED HISTORY ANALYSIS

Calder Walton

The outbreak of the war in Ukraine in February 2022 constitutes a staggering intelligence success for British and US agencies. 'Intelligence' and 'success' are two words that are not often heard together, not least because it is usually failures, not successes, that appear in the public domain. Failures are sadly obvious for all to see, while intelligence successes often remain hidden from public view. Before Putin's war in Ukraine in 2022, the British and US intelligence communities collected and disseminated accurate, timely and relevant intelligence about the war plans of Russia's leader, Vladimir Putin, for Ukraine. They then decided to downgrade and publicly disseminate that intelligence, warning the world about Putin's war. Doing so was a gamble, but the intelligence proved to be accurate.

This was not the first time that Western intelligence agencies have declassified intelligence in the pursuit of foreign policy. This short chapter explores four case studies where they have done so successfully and unsuccessfully. It then derives lessons from those case studies – as applied history – to give six guidelines to governments for deciding whether to downgrade intelligence in order to advance their policy making.

The missiles of October

Our story starts six decades before the war in Ukraine. One of the most striking episodes in which the US government declassified intelligence, and used it for diplomatic purposes, occurred during the Cuban Missile Crisis of October 1962. This was one of the most dangerous moments of the Cold War – and indeed, one of the most dangerous moments in history. During the crisis, the world's two superpowers, East and West, stood on the edge of nuclear war and global atomic annihilation. The history of the Cuban Missile Crisis has been scrutinised by countless studies elsewhere, and books about it are still being published even now, six decades after the event, so its story need not be rehearsed here at length, beyond the relevant facts.[1]

The Soviet leader, Nikita Khrushchev, knew the Soviet Union was outgunned by the United States. Washington had a nuclear arsenal, and missiles capable of delivering nuclear weapons, which were vastly superior to the Soviet Union's. The much discussed 'missile gap' in Washington, which claimed that the US government was lagging behind Moscow in missiles, was nonsense. The new US president in 1960, John F Kennedy, probably knew – or at least should have known – from US intelligence briefings that his pre-election campaign claims about a 'missile gap' were ill-founded. He continued, however, to make those claims regardless.[2] Khrushchev's decision in the spring of 1962 to place missiles on the Soviet-friendly island of Cuba, about 90 miles off the Florida coast, was designed to equalise the nuclear imbalance between East and West: the US government could launch missiles capable of striking at the heart of the Soviet Union, but the latter could not do the same against the United States. As Khrushchev later recalled, placing nuclear weapons on Cuba, which were capable of striking at the American heartland, was designed to mirror US and NATO missiles stationed in Eastern Europe and Turkey that were ominously pointed towards Moscow. He wanted to give America a 'taste of its own medicine', and throw a hedgehog down Uncle Sam's pants. For Khrushchev, the crisis was never really about Cuba itself. Revealingly, in Soviet history it is known as the 'Caribbean crisis'. Rather, the standoff was an extension of Khrushchev's principal strategy, which lay in Europe: to get an advantageous settlement to the question of Berlin, a city divided between both sides of the Cold War, lying deep inside East Germany, and which Khrushchev wanted to be incorporated into the Soviet orbit. The Soviet premier's strategy was to use missiles in Cuba to pressure Kennedy into a settlement over Berlin.[3]

Intelligence was central to Kennedy's handling of the Cuban Missile Crisis. The first indication gained by the US government about Soviet missiles on Cuba occurred on 15 October 1962. The previous day, a CIA high-altitude U-2 spy plane managed to photograph missiles on the island. After overnight processing and analysis by the CIA's National Photographic Interpretation Center, the CIA briefed the White House. Thus began the 13-day-long crisis, in which Kennedy and Khrushchev stood eyeball to eyeball, playing nuclear brinkmanship.

Kennedy famously took inspiration during the crisis from Barbara Tuchman's study, *The Guns of August*, about how European powers marched blindly into the First World War. Applying that book's lessons – applying history – Kennedy knew the gravity of the decisions he had to make.

One of the most dramatic moments during the crisis occurred on 25 October at the United Nations General Assembly in New York. As millions watched on their television screens, the Kennedy administration publicly revealed intelligence it had about the Soviet weapons. The task for doing this fell to Adlai Stevenson, the US ambassador to the UN. Stevenson, a long-standing Democrat, a former presidential hopeful himself and now a steady Kennedy loyalist, was a mild-mannered man who usually shied away from confrontation. On this occasion, he did not. He directed his questions at the Soviet ambassador, Valerian Zorin, in a skilful attorney-like cross-examination: 'Do you, Ambassador Zorin, deny that the USSR has placed, and is placing, medium- and intermediate-range missiles and sites in Cuba? Yes or no – don't wait for the translation, yes or no?'[4] Zorin, squirming in his chair, had not received instructions from Moscow and was left fumbling for an answer. 'I am not in an American courtroom, sir…You will have your answer in due course,' he said. Watching it on television in the White House, Kennedy telephoned a code-word – 'Stick it to him' – to Stevenson's team at the UN to declassify the U-2 intelligence showing the Soviet missiles in Cuba. Twisting the knife, Stevenson replied to Zorin: 'I am prepared to wait until Hell freezes over, if that is your decision. I am also prepared to present the evidence in this room.'

Waiting for laughter in the General Assembly to subside, Stevenson then produced his *coup de grâce*, the evidence for which the world had been waiting. He unveiled a series of black-and-white poster-sized photographs, which eviscerated Khrushchev's claim that the Soviet Union had not placed offensive weapons in Cuba. The whole assembly, and the world's media, could understand the significance of the canvas-coloured missile tubes revealed in the low-altitude images displayed. Zorin, now utterly befuddled, was left to claim that the images had been 'falsified' by the 'US intelligence service'.[5]

Kennedy's decision to disclose U-2 imagery intelligence (IMINT) was a central part of his propaganda campaign to win over world opinion and lay groundwork at the UN for a possible US invasion of Cuba, if that should prove necessary. It was successful. Until that point, many European audiences, who had been living under the shadow of nuclear war, did not necessarily see why Americans were so concerned about missiles capable of striking the United States. Seeing the actual Soviet missiles was, however, another matter. Kennedy's decision to downgrade the U-2 intelligence was also based on a calculation of balancing the benefits of doing so with the risk of jeopardising sources and methods. Back in May 1960, before Kennedy had become president, the Soviets had managed to shoot down a U-2 spy plane flying over the Soviet Union, piloted by Francis Gary Powers. The existence of the U-2 spy plane programme was thus already known to the Kremlin. That plane was downed by a missile, and it is safe to say that whatever on-board imagery capabilities the Soviet authorities were able to retrieve, they did not get them all. Kennedy therefore did not know precisely what the Soviets knew about the U-2. He evidently judged that the risk of betraying any still-secret U-2 capabilities were outweighed by the benefits to public diplomacy, during the crisis, of disclosing images obtained. Although documentary evidence is incomplete, it is possible that the U-2 images displayed at the UN were not the highest resolution IMINT capabilities of the spy plane.

Kennedy's calculation was surely correct. After seeing the images showing that Moscow had turned Cuba into a nuclear launch platform, world opinion was with Kennedy's administration. The crisis was resolved soon after, when Khrushchev decided to back down and Kennedy secretly agreed to remove US/NATO missiles from Turkey in exchange for Moscow removing its missiles from Cuba.[6]

Declassifying a mid-air shoot-down

Another crisis moment of the Cold War occurred on 1 September 1983, when a Soviet fighter plane shot down a Korean passenger Boeing 747 jumbo jet, KAL 007, travelling from New York to Seoul via Anchorage. The plane had blundered badly off course over Soviet airspace. The Soviet fighter shot it down apparently believing it was a US military aircraft. All 269 people on board were killed, including a US congressman, Lawrence 'Larry' McDonald. The news shocked the US president, Ronald Reagan, and his Secretary of State, George Shultz. To them, it was as if the Soviet Union, which Reagan had famously labelled the 'Evil Empire', had shown its true colours.[7]

From left, US Secretary of State George P
Shultz, National Security Advisor-designate
Robert McFarlane and President Ronald
Reagan on board Air Force One, 1983.

Reagan's administration responded to the shoot-down by declassifying intelligence about it – doing so too hastily, it turned out. Its intelligence on the shoot-down arose from signals intelligence (SIGINT) obtained by the National Security Agency (NSA). From listening posts in Japan, the NSA had managed to intercept a communication from the Soviet fighter pilot, in which he announced that he had fired on and destroyed the target. On the morning of 1 September in Washington – the same date the plane was blown up, allowing for time change – Shultz, with Reagan's blessing, went public with the incriminating SIGINT. Visibly angry and waving an intelligence report, Shultz told an assembled press conference at the State Department that the Soviet fighter could not have failed to realise it was a civilian aircraft. The Soviets had thus killed hundreds of civilian passengers in cold blood, he claimed. The SIGINT showed that Soviet radar had tracked the plane for two hours.

It was the first time a US Secretary of State had publicly referred to SIGINT to make a policy decision. The Reagan administration, however, undermined its powerful case against the Soviet Union by overstating it. In fact, as the historian Matthew Aid has shown, the 'solutions' or decrypted SIGINT, that Shultz had rushed to publicise were not yet finalised. When Shultz was disclosing them on 1 September, the NSA was actually still translating material and analysing it. When, later that day, the NSA completed its translation of the intercepts, they revealed that the Soviet air force believed they were tracking an American military reconnaissance aircraft, not a civilian Boeing 747. In a closed hearing of the Senate Committee on Foreign Relations, senators were told that NSA analysts had in fact believed that the Soviet pilot did not know the target was a civilian airliner.[8]

None of this, however, stopped Reagan, who was never one to let facts get in the way of a good story. The president followed Shultz with his own televised address, delivered on Labor Day, 5 September. Reagan's address was highly misleading. It showed the charismatic, inspiring film-star president at his myopic and vain worst. Unhappy with the initial draft of his speech, which he read beside the White House pool, Reagan went to his study, still wearing his damp swimming trunks, laid a towel over the chair at his desk and rewrote it. That night, he declared on air that the attack was an 'act of barbarism, born of a society which wantonly disregards individual rights and the value of human life and seeks constantly to expand and dominate other nations'. He played three carefully selected extracts of the audio decrypts to depict the Soviets in the worst possible light, as murderers. The US ambassador at the UN, Jeane Kirkpatrick, delivered a similarly misleading audio-visual presentation before the General Assembly of the plane being shot down, again using carefully extracted excerpts. (In retaliation, the KGB attempted to smear Kirkpatrick's reputation using forged documents.)[9]

At its headquarters in Fort Meade, Maryland, the NSA was aghast that its intelligence was being abused in this way by Reagan's White House. The NSA's deputy director of communications security, Walter Deeley, later vented his fury, growling that 'releasing the KAL material just for propaganda purposes cost us sources and gained nothing tangible in the long run'. Robert Gates, an officer at the Central Intelligence Agency (CIA) who would eventually become Director of Central Intelligence, would later politely but pointedly recall in his memoirs that 'the administration's rhetoric outran the facts known to it'.[10]

In Moscow, the reaction to the downing of the KAL 007 jet took a sadly predictable form, which made a terrible situation even worse: initial denial, followed by a torrent of misinformation, offering some facts while falsifying others, to make it seem that the US government was to blame for the disaster. Soviet state-press outlets reported that KAL 007 was an American spy plane, operated by the CIA, whose secret mission was espionage on Soviet territory. Dimitry Ustinov, a Marshal of the Soviet Union, and Viktor Chebrikov, KGB chairman, repeated this claim in a secret memorandum to leader Yuri Andropov. Nine days after KAL 007 was downed, Nikolai Ogarkov, chief of the Soviet general staff, held a press conference in which he asserted that the Korean passenger jet had deliberately strayed into Soviet territory. On 19 September, the KGB deputy chairman, Vladimir Kryuchkov, told the head of the East German Stasi that the Soviet pilots and ground control had genuinely thought it was a reconnaissance plane. Kryuchkov even outrageously suggested that, even though it was a civilian aircraft, it had been deliberately sent into Soviet airspace – to be shot down. Active KGB measures would continue to expose the truth, he said.[11]

In reality, there was no such conspiracy. The shoot-down of KAL 007 was a tragic, horrendous mistake – nothing more, nothing less. The significance of the episode for our purposes lies in what it reveals: the importance of intelligence being accurate before it is downgraded and publicly declassified. That may seem a blindingly obvious statement to make, but it bears emphasising: if the relevant intelligence is not accurate, disclosing it will at best be embarrassing, likely be counter productive and at worst turn the situation into a disaster.

A case study of failure: Iraq's weapons of mass destruction

The disaster scenario took place with the British and US governments' intelligence about Iraq's putative weapons of mass destruction (WMDs) in 2003. The story of London and Washington's mishandling of intelligence about Iraqi WMDs has now been exhaustively told elsewhere, and like the Cuban Missile Crisis above need not be replicated here. (Britain's official inquiry into Iraq, led by John Chilcot, comes in at 2.6 million words, longer than Tolstoy's *War and Peace*, the King James Bible and the complete works of Shakespeare). The eminent historian of the Cold War Melvyn Leffler has argued that there were understandable reasons why George W Bush's administration came to its decisions about WMDs based on the intelligence available. The chief of Britain's foreign intelligence service (SIS, or MI6) at the time, Sir Richard Dearlove, has recently claimed there is more to the story of intelligence and Iraq – but he was unable to disclose more details.[12]

In the absence of such information, the overall conclusion must remain: Anglo-American intelligence about Iraq's WMDs was a perfect storm of failure, a breakdown across the board in collection, analysis and dissemination. US and UK intelligence failed to collect reliable intelligence (relying heavily on a faulty single human source, code-named 'Curveball'), failed to analyse the collected data accurately (in essence, asking *where* the WMDs were, not *whether* there were any), and there was a breakdown in the nexus between intelligence agencies and decision-makers in London and Washington. There was insufficient distance between the former and the latter (exemplified by CIA director George Tenet's infamous 'slam dunk' comment in the Oval Office about WMDs, and the relaxed sofa-style government in Tony Blair's 10 Downing Street). As a result, intelligence agencies on both sides of the Atlantic failed in their primary mission: to provide objective assessments to decision-makers, 'to tell truth to power'. In a secret British government memorandum of July 2002, MI6 chief Dearlove relayed that

American troops dismantle the statue of
Saddam Hussein on Al-Firdos Square in
Baghdad, Iraq, 2003.

the Bush administration was 'fixing' the intelligence and facts to its already decided policy – to go to war to remove Saddam Hussein from power.[13]

In February 2003 the US Secretary of State, Colin Powell, briefed the United Nations about Iraq's WMDs. It was an infamous briefing, which became a blot on Powell's otherwise outstanding reputation. Much like Adlai Stevenson at the UN four decades earlier, Powell relied heavily on intelligence declassified for his speech. But unlike Stevenson's presentation before the Assembly, the intelligence that Powell relied on turned out to be faulty. It was a catastrophe. It meant that one of the principal reasons for the US government invading Iraq – to bring it 'freedom' and 'democracy' – was based on erroneous grounds. It also significantly damaged the public reputation of US and British intelligence. Iraq remains arguably the clearest example of the risks of governments declassifying intelligence.[14]

Declassifying Putin's war plans

US and British intelligence successfully unlocked and exposed Putin's war plans before his invasion of Ukraine in February 2022. This was a striking success for both intelligence communities, whose reputations were still living under the shadow of the Iraqi WMDs. It is not publicly known how the British and US were so successful at discovering Putin's intentions – nor should we know at this moment, while the war is still raging, for the protection of sources and methods. Public reporting suggests, however, that Russian troop communications were in some instances spectacularly insecure, which would have made them easy prey for US and British eavesdroppers at the NSA and the Government Communications Headquarters (GCHQ). Understanding Putin's intentions for Ukraine also suggests human intelligence, for Putin famously does not use email and the like. Public reporting indicates that the CIA was previously able to recruit an agent close to Putin himself.[15]

As the intelligence about Putin's war plans came into sharp focus in the summer and autumn of 2021, President Joe Biden's administration dispatched its most senior intelligence officials to warn European allies, not least Ukraine's leader, Volodymyr Zelenskyy, himself. The director of National Intelligence, Avril Haines, the head of the US intelligence community, travelled to Europe to alert leaders to the intelligence obtained about Putin's war plans. So did the Director of the CIA, William Burns, a veteran US diplomat with deep expertise on Russia, who in November 2021 also travelled to Moscow itself, where he reportedly warned Putin that the US knew about his plans for Ukraine. As a career consumer and user of intelligence, who was now on the other side of the table, producing intelligence, it may have been Burns who took an instrumental role in its declassification. At the time of writing, we do not know why such warnings did not dissuade Putin from his invasion. That will only be known if, or when, Russian records are made available, or a defector reveals the nature of Putin's decision-making before the invasion. (Those secrets may already be known to Western intelligence agencies.)[16]

Although matters must thus necessarily remain speculative for now, it seems probable that Putin's chauvinism about Ukraine, whose independence he disdained, would have warped his views about Ukraine's ability to defend itself. The systemic corruption of Russia's intelligence services also likely prevented them collecting reliable intelligence from inside Ukraine and effectively preparing for Russia's invasion. Like the worst of his predecessors in the Kremlin, the murderous nature of Putin's rule also guaranteed that he was given intelligence which confirmed rather than challenged his thinking. As with Stalin before him, telling truth to power in Putin's court – suggesting that the leader, *vozhd*, was wrong – was a career- and sometimes life-shortening decision for Russian intelligence officers, who have a tendency, like Putin's political opponents, to fall from windows and suffer otherwise untimely ends.

Zelenskyy himself was sceptical about warnings from London and Washington regarding Putin's war plans. This was understandable. Russia's military had previously surged forces near the Ukrainian border in what turned out to be false alarms. But in this instance, there were indicators that Russia's military was preparing for something different: the deployment of surgeons and blood banks to the areas near the Ukrainian border, which Russian forces had not previously done, suggested that they would indeed be embarking on an actual war.

In February 2022, the US and British governments took the bold decision to downgrade their intelligence and publicly warn about Putin's plans. 'It was too important to keep secret,' as one senior US intelligence official told me, on the condition of anonymity. Doing so was a gamble, for if their intelligence had been wrong, they would have faced a repetition of the WMD fiasco. But the intelligence turned out to be accurate.

February 1, 2022

President Volodymyr Zelenskyy and British Prime Minister Boris Johnson at a joint conference in Kyiv, February 2022.

According to two US intelligence officials intimately involved with the process of declassifying US intelligence about Ukraine, who again wish to remain anonymous, the availability of open source and commercially available intelligence was a 'game changer' for the capability of the US intelligence community. Private sector intelligence satellite providers, like Maxar Technologies, allowed the US intelligence community to find similar intelligence – imagery intelligence, IMINT – and declassify it without risking government sources and methods.[17]

Publicising the intelligence did not prevent Putin's decision to invade Ukraine. It does seem, however, to have derailed the invasion plans. London and Washington's warnings included details about Putin's concocted pretexts, or 'false flags', for invading Ukraine. With excuses for launching hostilities thus removed, Putin's forces failed in their primary objective: to take Kyiv. To the surprise of everyone apart from themselves, Ukrainians mounted a staggeringly brave defence of their country. Russia's combat forces, expecting a quick victory, and in some instances equipped with only a few days' rations, were forced to dig in for a long war of attrition. Thanks to Putin, the world now faced what most people believed had been relegated to a bygone era: a land war in Europe.

Conclusion: application of history

The recent explosion of intelligence from open and commercial sources constitutes a watershed in the history of intelligence and national security. They will continue to make it easier for governments to declassify intelligence than it previously was. Given this new environment, it seems advisable to establish guidelines for how and when intelligence can be downgraded for public consumption.

As the scholar Jay Mens has recently shown, there is no set methodology for the application of history for policy making.[18] The past does not offer up a list of ingredients, which can simply be mixed together and served up. The historian John Bew has noted – before he became a British foreign policy adviser – that history does not lend itself to PowerPoints or executive summaries.[19] It will not come as a surprise to readers of these pages, however, to hear that applying history is not futile. Pulling together the various threads of the above case studies, we can establish six policy guidelines for how intelligence can be effectively released for public audiences:

1. The declassification of intelligence must support clear, defined policy objectives;
2. The intelligence must be accurate, relevant, and timely;
3. Declassification does not, so far as possible, betray intelligence sources and methods;
4. If sources and methods are jeopardised (3., above), the foreign policy advantages of declassification must outweigh the security advantages for sources and methods remaining classified;
5. Partners and allies agree with declassifying the intelligence; and
6. The declassification process must be coordinated between different agencies and stakeholders.

The above guidelines are intended not to be prescriptive, but as a useful checklist for decision-makers when considering whether or not to declassify intelligence. Given the new digitally connected world in which we all now live, with exponentially more information available each day at the click of a mouse, there will correspondingly be increasing opportunities for governments to release intelligence through private sector providers. They now offer capabilities that, until recently, would have been the prized secrets of governments and intelligence communities.

1. See, for example, Serhii Plokhy, *Nuclear Folly: a History of the Cuban Missile Crisis.* New York: W.W. Norton, 2021.
2. For discussion, see Calder Walton, *Spies: the Epic Intelligence War between East and West.* New York: Simon & Schuster, 2023, ch 10.
3. For the 'Caribbean crisis', see Jonathan Haslam, *Near and Distant Neighbours: a New History of Soviet Intelligence.* Oxford: Oxford University Press, 2016, ch 8.
4. Dino Brugioni. *Eyeball to Eyeball: the Inside Story of the Cuban Missile Crisis.* New York: Random House, 1991, pp. 425–9.
5. Ibid.
6. Walton, *Spies*, ch 10.
7. Ibid. pp. 398–400.
8. Matthew Aid. *The Secret Sentry: the Untold History of the National Security Agency.* London: Bloomsbury, 2009, ch 10.
9. Ronald Reagan. *An American Life: the Autobiography.* New York: Simon & Schuster, 1990, pp. 583–4; Walton, *Spies*, pp. 398–400.
10. Robert Gates. *From the Shadows: the Ultimate Insider's Story of Five Presidents and How they Won the Cold War.* New York: Simon & Schuster, 2007, p. 268.
11. Walton, *Spies*, p. 400.
12. Melvyn Leffler. *Confronting Saddam Hussein: George W Bush and the Invasion of Iraq.* Oxford: Oxford University Press, 2022; for Dearlove's comments, see the BBC Radio 4 series *Shock and War: Iraq 20 Years On*, presented by Gordon Corera, March 2023, available here: https:www.bbc.co.uk/programmes/m001koc.
13. *The Report of the Iraq Inquiry* (2016) vol 2, p. 63, available here: https:assets.publishing.service.gov.uk/media/5a80b6a640f0b62302695161/The_Report_of_the_Iraq_Inquiry_-_Volume_II.pdf.
14. President George W Bush has recently emphasised that his 'war on terror' was driven by a strategy to bring 'democracy' and 'freedom' to countries in the Middle East: see his Foreword in Stephen J Hadley (ed.), with Peter Feaver, William Inboden and Meghan L O'Sullivan (co-eds.), *Hand-Off: theForeign Policy George W Bush Passed to Barack Obama.* Washington DC: Brookings Institution Press, 2022.
15. Julian Barnes, Adam Goldman and David E Sanger. CIA Informant extracted from Russia had sent secrets to Russia for decades. *New York Times*, 17 September 2019.
16. Julian Barnes and Helene Cooper. US battles Putin by disclosing his next possible moves. *New York Times.* 13 February 2022; Jim Lawless and Aamer Madhani. Secret intelligence has unusually public role in Ukraine war. *AP News*, 3 April 2022.
17. Unattributable author interview with two US intelligence officers, 3 May 2022 and 15 November 2023.
18. Jay Mens. Two types of applied history. *Journal of Applied History.* December 2023.
19. John Bew. United Kingdom: the best education, in The Big Question: What Lessons from History Keep being Forgotten? *World Policy Institute.* Fall 2016, available through Duke University Press website.

Mao Zedong, founder of the
People's Republic of China, 1960.

PROBLEMATIC ASSUMPTIONS IN US INTELLIGENCE ON CHINA IN THE EARLY COLD WAR

Sara Bush Castro[1]

Intelligence seeks to help leaders overcome uncertainty in national security decision-making. This goal involves the endeavour to provide actionable and confident responses to the most difficult questions leaders encounter. Intelligence analysts often describe their work as similar to tackling a jigsaw puzzle while coping with the doubt that you have all the pieces you need, lacking confidence that all the pieces you have actually belong in your puzzle, and without the advantage of the broad picture the puzzle intends to display. Eliminating all uncertainty in this work is impossible. Flaws, dead ends and lacunae are an inevitable part of the intelligence process. In some cases, such issues can lead to serious consequences for policy outcomes.

One important lesson that the history of known intelligence failures has revealed is that foundational assumptions carry heavy weight in both collection and analysis. Assumptions about targets shape intelligence taskings and results. Skewed assumptions can easily focus resources in the wrong direction.

Declassified examples of US intelligence about the People's Republic of China (PRC) in the early Cold War – the 1950s and 1960s – offer a powerful depiction of this lesson. In this case, US intelligence officers assumed that Communist China lacked the ability to independently develop modernised military capabilities, especially nuclear weapons. They were certain the Chinese Communist Party (CCP) required Soviet assistance to achieve its military goals. Paternalistic US perceptions about China's backwardness fed the hypothesis. But this assumption turned out to be incorrect, and it precipitated a cascade of flawed intelligence assessments leading up to China's successful test of a Chinese-designed nuclear bomb in 1964. Due to confirmation bias, the use of high-tech tools, such as the U-2 high-altitude reconnaissance aircraft, tended to reinforce US confidence in intelligence assessments rather than introduce doubt.

Approximately two months before Lockheed test pilot Tony LeVier took the first U-2 on its maiden voyage in August 1955, the Central Intelligence Agency (CIA) was already facing questions from policy-makers about China's intentions and capabilities. The question of China's potential access to nuclear weapons weighed heavily on US China watchers at the time. In June 1955, the CIA published an assessment to address the questions. Well-respected CIA intelligence analyst Sherman Kent, after whom the CIA's analytic training school is currently named, introduced the estimate, directing his preface squarely on the potential nuclearisation of the PRC.[2] Kent wrote:

> Communist China almost certainly could not develop significant capabilities for the production of nuclear weapons within the next 10 years unless it were given substantial external assistance. Without such assistance, the development of an adequate industrial base and a supply of trained scientific and technical personnel sufficient to support an effective nuclear weapons program would probably take well over 10, and possibly 20 years.

This estimate turned out to be flawed in both assumptions and conclusions. This essay explores the reasons behind the flawed assumptions and how they contributed to skewed conclusions, even as the US adopted more sophisticated methods for intelligence collection, such as high-altitude overhead reconnaissance.

At the same time as Kent was supervising the drafting of the National Intelligence Estimate (NIE) and Lockheed's Skunk Works were in the final stages of developing the U-2 aircraft, discussions of implementing a nuclear weapons programme were already under way among CCP leaders in Beijing. In 1954, a year before Kent's assessment, CCP leader Mao Zedong had issued a secret directive within the People's Liberation Army (PLA) to gather Chinese scientists and begin establishing a nuclear weapons programme, independent from Soviet aid if necessary.[3] By April 1956, the PLA team had sufficient momentum that Mao Zedong spoke about his intentions at an enlarged meeting of the CCP Central Politburo, urging changes to fiscal policy that could support the continuation of the nuclear weapons development programme. In the speech, Mao argued that having a nuclear weapon was a necessary deterrent in the post-Second World War world:

We still don't have the atomic bomb, but in the past we didn't have airplanes or artillery either. We relied on millet and rifles to defeat the Japanese imperialists and Chiang Kai-shek. Now we're already stronger than we were in the past, and in the future we'll be even stronger than now. Not only are we going to have more airplanes and artillery, but also the atomic bomb. In today's world, if we don't want to be bullied, we have to have this thing.[4]

The CCP under Mao determined that a nuclear weapon would provide an undeniable deterrent to both the United States and the Soviet Union, should either state encroach on Chinese sovereignty.

Mao was prepared to go to extreme measures to ensure China developed this capability. China held out hope for Soviet aid to their nuclear weapons programme for the first few years, but soon abandoned their optimism. Instead, the Party rounded up Chinese scientists who had studied physics, engineering and chemistry either at top Chinese universities or abroad with world-famous scholars. Prior to the Second World War, many Chinese scholars had sought advanced degrees abroad, and many of them had ended up working in laboratories performing research at the cutting edge of nuclear physics. For example, the scientist who the PRC later declared to be the 'father of the atomic bomb' in China, Deng Jiaxian, earned his doctorate at Purdue University in the United States in 1950 with a dissertation titled 'The Photo-Disintegration of the Deuteron'.[5] Deng was among a group of scientists with similar credentials in China in the 1950s.[6] Together they independently developed a nuclear payload using enriched uranium. They also developed the entire supply chain and machines required for producing the weapon while maintaining tight operational security and active campaigns of denial and deception.

On 16 October 1964, the PRC celebrated detonating its first nuclear device at the remote Lop Nur test site in Xinjiang, China's far western province.[7] The bomb used uranium-235 that Chinese scientists had mined and enriched within China to trigger a fission implosion, yielding a 20-kiloton explosive reaction that they had exclusively engineered. By this time, US intelligence officials had updated their assessments, reporting to policymakers that China was pursuing nuclear technology for both energy production and weapons development. These assessments were based in part on expensive high-altitude overhead reconnaissance. By 1964, the CIA anticipated that a PRC nuclear bomb test could happen at any time.[8] However, China's methods for developing this successful bomb contradicted the most important assumptions US intelligence analysis had made about Chinese capabilities, even with the benefit of overhead imagery.

The precision of high-altitude imagery intelligence and the technical achievement it represented to US national security officials may have contributed to a false sense of confidence among American intelligence officials focused on China. The problem was not the technology; it was the humans interacting with it and the set of foundational assumptions from which they proceeded. In fact, high-altitude surveillance did not quite deliver the intelligence on the PRC to US policymakers that the engineers had promised, sometimes because of structural constraints (including unavoidable issues like orbital range and the weather) but largely because of the nascency of effective intelligence analysis. Furthermore, the heavy US expenditures and regular overflights appear to have contributed to an increase in defensive action from Chinese leaders, particularly denial and deception efforts that made the PRC an even harder target for US intelligence than it already was during the early Cold War.

US intelligence assessments of the PRC from the 1950s and 1960s show a clear pattern of underestimating China's technical and military capabilities that reflects what historian Michael H Hunt described in his classic 1983 book as the 'special relationship' many Americans believed the United States had with China. Much different to the 'special relationship' between the US and the United Kingdom that many intelligence historians describe, the US vision of a special relationship with China dated from the first American contact with China in the 18th century. In this view, the United States had a role to play in sharing its liberal values with China, edging out the less honourable goals of European imperialists who dominated much of the country during what Chinese president Xi Jinping today dubs China's 'century of humiliation' – a period spanning roughly from China's defeat in the Opium Wars of the 1840s to China's occupation by Japan into the 1940s. Hunt argues that a paternalistic 'open door constituency' of Americans 'propagated a vision of defending and reforming China' that intrinsically assumed a lack of Chinese capability for self-reform and which required the assistance of the superior United States whether or not China sought it.[9]

Workers and technicians at the Lop Nur nuclear
weapons test base, Xinjiang, celebrate China's
first nuclear bomb explosion, 1964.

More recently, Zach Fredman has argued that the Second World War, during which the United States and China were allies, represented a shift in American attitudes towards a 'post-imperial mode of domination and wielding power', in evidence in the tone of US intelligence reporting on China's nuclear programme in the 1950s and 1960s.[10] The vital role of American air power in Second World War successes contributed to the sentiment that Americans 'could fly anything anywhere anytime'.[11] This attitude, which historian Kristie Macrakis has referred to as 'technophilia', pervaded the development of the modern US national security regime during the Truman and Eisenhower presidencies.[12] US intelligence assessments of China's nuclearisation that have become public bear the signs of both open-door paternalism and technophilia having a warping effect on US intelligence perceptions of China's capabilities.

US intelligence assessments generally underestimated the speed and progress of China's nuclear programme. Declassified US intelligence assessments from the 1950s reveal intelligence officials admitting significant gaps in their knowledge about the People's Republic but nonetheless advancing opinions about the possibilities for Chinese nuclear weapons development that were based on perceptions of Soviet intentions and cultural assumptions about China. Certainty that the Chinese nuclear programme would require Soviet aid informed the collection assignments for U-2 planes and probably prevented US intelligence officials from exploring or describing to policymakers the alternative paths to an atomic payload, such as the one China's nuclear scientists ultimately followed.

Between 1955 and the successful Chinese bomb test in 1964, US intelligence estimates home in on China's increasing potential for reaching the testing milestone, but the included reasoning reveals intelligence gaps and analytical errors. For example, a National Intelligence Estimate published in 1958 anticipated Mao's crucial shift in strategy to emphasise military modernisation and deterrence, based on a close reading of Chinese state-run mass media and a handful of other sources. However, this data did not budge the CIA's confidence that China's potential for nuclear weapons production was limited without Soviet aid:

Although Communist China will almost certainly not have developed a missile or nuclear weapons production capability of its own by 1962 because of the continuing shortage of technicians and the demands of other military and economic programs upon its limited resources, we believe that the Chinese Communists will press the USSR for such advanced weapons.[13]

Records available today reveal two important deviations between this assessment and what actually happened in China. First, Mao's discontent with Khrushchev reached fever pitch, and China cut its ties with the Soviet Union. The Soviets did give the CCP SA-2 missiles that the PLA used to shoot down U-2s, but they never provided any significant aid to China's nuclear programme. Soviet aid to China's nuclear weapons programme after 1960 was extremely unlikely. Second, the team of nuclear scientists the PLA had gathered following Mao's secret directive to start the nuclear programme in 1954 were well along in developing a supply chain and procedure for enriching uranium.[14] CIA officials with expertise on nuclear weapons would likely have known that some of the details for the process of enriching uranium had even become public by the mid-1950s.[15] Mao's select group of Chinese scientists capitalised on such information and combined it with their expertise. They laboured on with state protections for their work and provisions for resources, even through the chaos of Mao's brutal campaigns for economic and social revolution in the late 1950s.

The facilities for enriching uranium do not conform to the signatures, structures or supply chain nodes required for Soviet-style plutonium production. Given CIA analysts' deep conviction that China could only develop a nuclear weapon with Soviet aid, they likewise assumed China would be producing plutonium with a Soviet recipe to develop a bomb. The CIA thus directed high-altitude overflights to seek indicators of plutonium production. Failure to locate indicators of this production process encouraged them to think China's nuclear project was much less advanced than it actually was. Relaxing assumptions about China's capabilities could have led US intelligence analysts in the 1950s to target overhead imagery collection of different indicators. Instead, they directed assets at particular indicators that would have only been present in a Soviet-style nuclear programme, such as the signatures of plutonium. Because China independently developed its payload using enriched uranium, US intelligence collection failed to detect the signatures of a Soviet-style programme, missing the active development of the enriched uranium payload in the process. The lack of evidence reinforced a confirmation bias: US intelligence officials determined that the nuclear programme must not exist when they could not find it even with multiple high-risk U-2 overflights.

In the 1950s, the CIA employed many talented and capable researchers and analysts, but the field of intelligence analysis was quite new. Analysts were not taught the same kind of rigorous tradecraft employed today. Current techniques evolved through trial and error over decades of CIA work, with some major strides not coming until the 21st century in the aftermath of the Iraq weapons of mass destruction intelligence failure. Intelligence assessments about the PRC faced additional challenges beyond the nascency of the analytic tradecraft. Many among the cohort of subject matter experts (SMEs) on China and East Asia who had participated in wartime US intelligence efforts left civilian public service in the 1950s. Even if these SMEs had remained at the CIA, they could still have been a source of the open-door paternalism that put a culturally biased tinge on intelligence analysis. However, the SMEs also spoke Chinese and many had lived in China for years before and during the Second World War. Their familiarity with and expertise on China's history, politics and culture might have improved US intelligence collection and analysis. However, wartime demobilisation and the reorganisation of US national security assets under the National Security Act of 1947 itself encouraged China SMEs to leave the government and filter into other ventures. In the 1950s, political outcomes in China that led to the establishment of the Communist-led PRC drove questions about the loyalty of US experts on China. Senator Joseph McCarthy's inquiries in 1953 and 1954 – the same years that Mao was starting China's nuclear programme and Lockheed Skunk Works engineers were developing the U-2 aircraft – made negative examples of some of the most prominent China experts, such as John Service, John Paton Davies and Owen Lattimore. It would be difficult indeed to use public records to document with confidence the numbers of American wartime China SMEs who continued to work at the CIA during and immediately after McCarthy's inquiries. However, the memoirs and correspondence of those who came into McCarthy's focus strongly suggest the hearings had a chilling effect on the CIA's retention of these experts.

Human intelligence (HUMINT) could have balanced out some of the conclusions analysts drew from the use of the new tools for overhead surveillance, but the US government struggled to effectively collect human intelligence on China in the 1950s. The closure of the Chinese mainland to most American citizens between 1949 and 1979 due to the lack of normalised diplomatic relations between the United States and the PRC reduced the capacity for the US government to collect vital HUMINT, whether via overt or clandestine methods. American diplomats and attachés posted to the US embassy and other diplomatic outposts on the Chinese mainland in the 1930s and early 1940s had established a norm for overt HUMINT collection in the course of their normal job duties representing the interests of the United States in China. Embassy staff regularly recorded notes of their meetings, interviews and observations of Chinese nationals and dispatched them back to the State Department headquarters.[16] After the establishment of the PRC in 1949, the US embassy moved to Taiwan, and Americans were no longer free to travel in China. The US government lost its biggest window into Chinese society. Clandestine HUMINT collection remained possible in China, but it was challenging, dangerous and rare. More extensive HUMINT reporting might have cast doubt earlier on the core assumption CIA analysts made that China needed Soviet help to achieve a nuclear weapons programme.

The limitation of closed borders for US intelligence in the early Cold War combined with the pervasive sense of technophilia within the US national security regime in the 1950s to prompt massive US expenditure on tools for high-altitude overhead intelligence collection. American policymakers opened up the budget to accommodate the high price tag of developing new tools for technical espionage. President Eisenhower designated $35 million for the CIA to order the first 20 U-2 planes from Lockheed in 1954.[17] Adjusted for inflation, this amount would be equal to around $331m today. The original contract for developing the A-12 OXCART in 1960 was for $96.6m (equivalent to $9.8 billion today), and the actual costs ended up being double that amount due to the expense of the A-12's titanium frame.[18] These numbers were just for the development and the planes. Once operational, these airframes also carried costs for pilots, maintenance, fuel, parts and other human resources support.

The introduction of such substantial budgetary requirements to support the engineering and deployment of these tools occurred in parallel with an expansion of government and military organisations that would use them. The National Security Act of 1947 established the CIA and the Air Force, and soon came the National Security Agency (1952) and

National Reconnaissance Office (1960). Today's National Geospatial-Intelligence Agency grew out of a constellation of smaller organisations – such as the National Photographic Interpretation Center – that sprouted up after 1960 to support the new surveillance tools in which the United States had invested.

US national security decision-makers were generally happy to justify these expenses, due to their confidence in American air power. They claimed intelligence collected through overhead reconnaissance was superior to old-fashioned HUMINT and open-source analysis because it was more precise, more accurate and safer for personnel. The case of intelligence on China's nuclearisation challenged all three of these arguments. U-2 photos were precise and accurate but, as already described, they had to be directed at the right targets to be able to yield actionable and correct results. The Chinese case also created diplomatic and physical danger for pilots.

Because the Eisenhower administration worried about the diplomatic consequences of US pilots overflying denied airspace, as early as 1951 the US expanded its collaboration with the Taiwan-based Republic of China Air Force (ROCAF).[19] At the time, the CIA and US Air Force were collaborating with Chinese Nationalists on Taiwan to deploy covert air reconnaissance and imagery collection missions over mainland China.[20] US advisers partnered with the ROCAF to form, equip and train that force's 34th and 35th squadrons.[21] These units operated under heavy secrecy and, in the 1960s, they were known colloquially as the Black Bats and Black Cats, respectively. The US government relied on these ROCAF units throughout the 1950s and 1960s to aid collection of secret imagery and other intelligence on China's military modernisation and developing nuclear weapons programme.

As of August 1953, the US National Security Council and the CIA had determined that having US personnel pilot overflights of China or Russia was too risky to be standard operating procedure because it was too difficult to maintain the plausible deniability the United States desired for its covert missions.[22] Casualties or high-profile aircraft loss would harm diplomatic efforts and might have an impact on domestic public opinion. The CIA exploited a few exceptions to the ban on US overflight pilots in the 1950s and 1960s, but with the ROCAF willing to co-operate and to provide capable pilots, training ROCAF personnel to fly U-2s was a natural move. Starting in 1961, ROCAF pilots flew aerial reconnaissance flights over China using U-2 aircraft that the US government supplied in a now declassified series of operations.[23] Taiwanese ROCAF pilots operated the U-2s that flew over China, including the five the PRC shot down with Soviet SA-2 missiles. ROCAF pilots in the missions routinely carried both gold bars for bribes and cyanide capsules for suicide, in anticipation of being shot down.[24]

The CCP detected aerial surveillance by the United States, and this prompted defensive counter intelligence measures towards the nuclear programme. Declassified records about the ROCAF Black Cat squadrons document pilot knowledge that the CCP military were well aware of overflights for the entire time they were occurring. Historians have noted that PRC leaders took extreme deceptive measures to protect their nuclear programme supply chain. For example, buildings needed for stockpiling and enriching the uranium that became China's first nuclear bomb were hidden in plain sight in industrial parks within the small cities of Henan and Hebei provinces. When time came to test the weapon and it was no longer possible to conceal the effort from overhead imagery, CCP leaders intensified their efforts by locating the test site deep in the Taklamakan Desert in China's north-west region of Xinjiang, making it impossible for even long-distance U-2 planes to fly from Taiwan or Japan all the way across China, take photographs and return on one tank of fuel. CCP leaders may have been prepared to take these defensive measures against US reconnaissance operations anyway, but the regularity and intensity of aerial overflights would not have encouraged the PLA to let down its guard.

In the case of US intelligence estimates about the progress of China's nuclear weapons programme in the 1950s, preformed attitudes about Chinese capabilities conspired with other circumstances of US intelligence collection and analysis to produce flawed assessments. This historical case emphasises the dangers of placing too much confidence in any one information stream. It also highlights how cultural impressions and attitudes can wield influence over analysis, even when analysts are attempting to employ evidence-based tradecraft.

The estimates described in this essay are nearly 70 years old. In the context of studying intelligence failures, it is certainly worth asking how many of the problematic circumstances that intelligence analysts faced in the 1950s and 1960s have changed in today's environment.

In conclusion, comparing declassified US intelligence estimates on China in the 1950s and 1960s with credible historical records that have emerged from China about its nuclear weapons development emphasises a sustained pattern of problematic underestimation of Chinese technical capabilities by US intelligence.

1. The views expressed are those of the author and do not reflect the official policy or position of the US Department of Defense, the US Government, the US Air Force Academy or the US Air Force.
2. Russell Lee. A high-flying spy plane. National Air and Space Museum, 26 April 2019, https:airandspace.si.edu/stories/editorial/high-flying-spy-plane; Sherman Kent, AD/N. Memorandum for the Director, Subject: Chinese Communist capabilities for developing an effective atomic weapons program and weapons delivery program, 24 June 1955, online via CIA Reading Room, https:www.cia.gov/readingroom/docs/CIA-RDP79R00904A000200030014-1.pdf.
3. William Burr and Jeffrey T Richelson. Whether to 'strangle the baby in the cradle': the United States and the Chinese nuclear program, 1960–1964. *International Security*, vol 23, no 3, 2000–1, p. 58.
4. Talk by Mao Zedong at an Enlarged Meeting of the Chinese Communist Party Central Committee Politburo (Excerpts). 25 April 1956, History and Public Policy Program Digital Archive, Mao Zedong wenji, vol 7. Beijing: Renmin Chubanshe, 1999, p. 27. Translated by Neil Silver.
5. Deng Jiaxian. The Photo-Disintegration of the Deuteron (PhD dissertation). Purdue University, Archives and Special Collections, https:archives.lib.purdue.edu/repositories/2/resources/1188.
6. For further on these Chinese scientists, see John Wilson Lewis and Xue Litai, *China Builds the Bomb*. Stanford: Stanford University Press, 1988, pp. 148–55.
7. Analysis of China's nuclear programme and what US intelligence analysts knew about it in the 1960s draws heavily on a previous article I wrote, published by the Wilson Center. See Sara Castro, Lop Nur and the US intelligence gaze: evaluating the US intelligence process during China's nuclearization, in Abraham M Denmark and Lucas Meyers (eds.), *2020–2021 Wilson China Fellowship Publication: Essays on the Rise of China and Its Implications*, 2021, https:www.wilsoncenter.org/publication/2020-21-wilson-china-fellowship-essays-rise-china-and-its-implications.
8. Burr and Richelson, Whether to 'strangle the baby in the cradle', p. 56.
9. Michael H Hunt. *The Making of a Special Relationship: the United States and China to 1914*. New York: Columbia University Press, 1983, p. xi.
10. Zach Fredman. *The Tormented Alliance: American Servicemen and the Occupation of China, 1941–1949*. Chapel Hill: University of North Carolina Press, 2022, p. 10.
11. Ibid, p. 1.
12. For further on technophilia and aerial espionage in the United States in the early Cold War, see Kristie Macrakis, *Nothing is Beyond Our Reach: America's Techno-Spy Empire*. Washington DC: Georgetown University Press, 2023, and Dino A Brugioni, *Eyes in the Sky: Eisenhower, the CIA, and Cold War Aerial Espionage*. Annapolis, MD: Naval Institute Press, 2010.
13. Director of Central Intelligence, National Intelligence Estimate 13–58: Communist China, 13 May 1958, republished in National Intelligence Council, *Tracking the Dragon: National Intelligence Estimates on China During the Era of Mao, 1948–1970*, n.p., 2004.

14. Burr and Richelson, Whether to 'strangle the baby in the cradle', p. 58.
15. Ibid.
16. Some records of this diplomatic activity are easily accessible in the US State Department's multi-volume series *Foreign Relations of the United States*, online at https:history.state.gov/historicaldocuments/ebooks.
17. Gregory W Pedlow and Donald E Welzenbach. *The Central Intelligence Agency and Overhead Reconnaissance: the U-2 and OXCART Programs, 1954–1974*. New York: Skyhorse, 2016, p. 52.
18. Ibid, p. 288.
19. Denied area overflights for the collection of strategic electronic intelligence, 26 August 1953, reproduced in R Cargill Hall and Clayton D Laurie, *Early Cold War Overflights: Symposium Proceedings*. Washington DC: Office of the Historian, National Reconnaissance Office, 2003, p. 491. https:babel.hathitrust.org/cgi/pt?id=nyp.33433032546263&view=1up&seq=7&skin=2021.
20. 'Chinese Nationalist' is the English translation of the official name of the 国民党 political party, Romanised as Kuomintang/KMT in Taiwan and Guomindang/GMD in the People's Republic. This paper uses the Taiwanese spelling to maintain consistency with the bulk of the source records for this project.
21. For more on the history of these squadrons, see Chris Pocock with Clarence Fu, *The Black Bats: CIA Spy Flights Over China from Taiwan, 1951–1969*. Atglen, PA: Schiffer Military History, 2010.
22. Denied area overflights, p. 491.
23. Jeffrey T Richelson. *Spying on the Bomb: American Nuclear Intelligence from Nazi Germany to Iran and North Korea*. New York: W W Norton, 2006, p. 146.
24. Pocock with Fu, *The Black Bats,* p. 8.

Israeli soldiers patrol the Kibbutz Be'eri
on the border with Gaza, October 2023.

ISRAEL'S INTELLIGENCE FAILURE
PRIOR TO 7 OCTOBER 2023

Steven Wagner

On 7 October 2023 the Islamic Resistance Movement, known by its acronym, Hamas, launched a surprise attack on Israeli border positions around Gaza, breaching high-tech defences and then pouring into Israeli communities, a music festival and an Israel Defence Forces (IDF) divisional headquarters, among other targets. Two months later, authorities were still identifying the remains of the approximately 1,250 dead. 254 were taken hostage, including about 24 soldiers. 135 have since been freed, 120 remain in Gaza, 43 of whom have been declared dead by the time of publication. In an effort to destroy Hamas, the IDF has occupied swathes of the Gaza Strip at the cost of tens of thousands of innocent Palestinians' lives. It is difficult to imagine what good might come of all this.

This assault began when, for two days, security in the Gaza envelope had collapsed. Hamas overcame several layers of automated detection systems in the air, on the ground and underground. These are monitored remotely and locally, passively and actively, and are defended with soldiers on the spot, from guard towers and remote-controlled machine guns. Hamas planned the operation meticulously, reconnoitring and choosing targets and tactics carefully. It is clear that preparations lasted some two years.

Hamas may have chosen the date for its auspicious 50-year anniversary of Israel's last disaster, the surprise attack of the Yom Kippur War. It is more likely, however, that the timing was chosen for tactical reasons. Guard duty on Saturday morning, especially on holidays (it was the end of the Sukkot festival), is generally seen by conscripts as likely to be quiet, and an undesirable obligation. The IDF garrison around Gaza had been weakened by events in the West Bank. Weeks prior, the 143 'Gaza' Division transferred three battalions to the West Bank to cover security during the holidays as Jewish settlers had planned provocative demonstrations. Left behind were three experienced but under-strength battalions – the storied 51st and 13th battalions of the Golani Brigade, and Sayeret Nahal, each of which suffered substantial losses – and the 33rd 'Caracal' Battalion, a new and experimental mixed-gender armoured battalion of the border defence corps, it turns out they killed civilians too. The rise of non-partisan Palestinian 'brigade' units in the Nablus–Tulkarem–Jenin area of the West Bank had been capturing the attention of Israeli security since at least 2021. The government and the IDF considered Hamas to be a lower security risk.

The question nags: how did Israel's security and intelligence services, with their legendary reputations, allow this to happen? How were the warning signs of a surprise attack missed? The events of 7 October 2023 resulted from a set of catastrophic failures of Israel's intelligence services and its political leadership. Intelligence failures affected analytic trade-craft, organisational structure and processes, approaches to briefing, sex-ism and rank bias, and a failure to disseminate. These are underpinned by obvious and overarching failures of leadership and policy. To date, no senior person in authority has resigned – and heads must roll to revive trust in the system.

It is vital that these failures are unpacked, even before a commission of inquiry has a chance to complete a formal process. What becomes appar-ent is that our idea of 'intelligence failure', in both scholarship and in the public sphere, is a woolly and analytically useless concept. It is important therefore that our examination of this case helps us to sharpen a concept which can be used to diagnose problems in the future. Intelligence profes-sionals, I argue, need to be judged on their processes more than on their results. Most scholarly approaches to failure depend on hindsight core to the historical craft but mostly worthless to organisational design. That said, there is emerging Israeli scholarship which suggests that Israeli defence intelligence – processed in the research and analysis department (RAD) of the intelligence branch of the general staff (AMAN) – is resist-ant to structuring its analytic craft or to aligning it with social-scientific methodology. Likewise, Israel lacks some of the processes, structures and doctrines which would allow raw intelligence to be scrutinised and weighed independently. These shortcomings must change.

What emerges is a razor, conceived around the notion of social-scientific replicability: an event is only considered 'intelligence failure' when the intelligence community fails to meet professional standards. If a change of intelligence personnel or process might produce a different result, the case is probably intelligence failure. If a change of leadership or policy could change the outcome, it's probably not intelligence failure.

Obviously this too requires counterfactual thinking, but it shifts the conversation away from a well-trodden path of 'blame' and towards diagnosis. There are also social-scientific solutions to these unknowable questions. Wargaming, modelling and simulation are promising examples of such solutions; incidentally, these are also useful tools for intelligence analysts who need to perform counterfactual analysis. My goal here is to break a long-standing pattern where, after failure, leaders blame intelligence and invest large sums of public money in reform designed to solve yesterday's problems instead of tomorrow's. Democratic accountability in Israel is already hanging by a thread following the prime minister's ten-month-long attempt to weaken the judiciary. Therefore, in order to achieve any kind of accountability for failure, Israel's commissioners will require a clear and useful concept of intelligence failure.

Before we examine the case and draw upon it for conceptual refinement, it is important to note that the evidence base for this case is fresh and incomplete. We rely almost exclusively on media reports from an environment with substantially more censorship and a more curated information environment than we are used to in the UK, EU and North America. Moreover, there have been a substantial number of leaks about intelligence failure in AMAN. These need to be handled carefully. I do not believe in conspiracy theories. My sense, today, is that the data which have been leaked are genuine, but that these have been chosen to keep Israeli media focused on the military's failure. It is possible that journalists simply got access to angry soldiers, but one would expect arrests and further scandal to follow unauthorised disclosure. It has not. We cannot know for sure, but healthy scepticism must join an understanding that the leaked information on intelligence failure on 7 October has been chosen for a reason.

Warning signs

At the time of writing (January 2024) there is already ample evidence that warning signs were missed. In the days following the massacre, Egypt's intelligence chief publicly announced that he had, ten days before the attack, personally warned Israeli prime minister Benjamin Netanyahu

Benjamin Netanyahu talks to the
media at the Israeli Defence Ministry,
within the Kirya, 12 October 2023.

that 'something big' was about to happen.[1] Netanyahu's office denied this, although the story has been confirmed by multiple outlets. Likewise, American sources began to buzz about both the Egyptian angle and their own intelligence community's evidence. Although American warning intelligence about Hamas does not seem to have risen to the national all-source assessment body, the National Intelligence Council (NIC), journalists cited specific evidence presented by senior intelligence officials. These warnings were raised with the White House, it would seem. One non-specific warning came from the CIA. The other American assessment, drawn from Israeli-shared source material, indicated 'unusual activity' by Hamas.[2] The general staff had offered a number of generic warnings that Israel's enemies were noting its internal strife and could choose to exploit it. We can infer from the rapid and unprecedented American response that it was well informed about the risk of escalation and spillover. This, by the way, is surely an American intelligence success story. To be sure, the deployment of two carrier groups and additional forces to the region was not for Hamas but for Iran and its regional partners, especially Hezbollah.

There is substantial information emerging from Israel too. Recently, the newspaper *Haaretz* reported on its interviews with surviving *tatzpitaniot*, women soldiers who serve as spotters on the Gaza border's watch and command and control apparatus. These survivors of the onslaught, whose comrades were killed and taken captive, went to the press to detail the range of warnings they had provided since at least early 2023. They observed Hamas carrying out drills with drones, showing off their knowledge of Israeli camera positions and drilling attacks on tanks, using paragliders, et cetera. Their warnings over these drills were especially salient over the four to six weeks before the attack. These women said that Hamas were the negligent ones: 'It didn't try to hide anything and its actions were out in the open.' They argue that a mix of sexism, rankism and organisational dysfunction led their warnings to go unheeded. The best summary came from one interviewee, who concluded that a veteran spotter 'does not need 8200 [Israel's signals intelligence unit] in order to tell immediately whether her sector is operating unusually'.[3] Alas, senior officers in the Gaza Division and military intelligence discounted their observations.

Information was also published showing that personnel within Unit 8200 of AMAN also warned of Hamas plans. It reported about Hamas drills and how they matched a document held by the unit, nicknamed 'Walls of Jericho', which outlined Hamas plans to strike Israeli border positions and civilian communities. The veteran analyst concluded: 'It is a plan to start a war…it's not just a raid on a village.'[4] The IDF held information that Hamas had been considering this kind of operation since 2016. The Gaza Division of the IDF, whose headquarters at Re'im were sacked on 7 October, believed the plan was aspirational but that Hamas lacked the capability. Unit 8200 has completed its own classified post-mortem, reviewed by journalist Ben Caspit. The report describes personnel issues, heaping praise on a woman non-commissioned officer (NCO), known as 'V', whose warnings went unheeded, and couching criticism of her superiors in a broader description of structural problems. It describes the introduction of new technology which pools intelligence data for analysts but which removed an erstwhile practice of 'pushing' assessments upon senior officers and decision-makers. Since data is pooled, analysts in AMAN, who often lack subject matter expertise, are required to 'pull' data and to know intuitively what queries to make. A junior analyst, who has since offered to resign, did not even know AMAN's technical term for traffic analysis data – 'contentless intelligence' – during the internal review. He thus missed key signals of unusual activity in Gaza before the attack.[5]

Analytic failures

Many of the problems identified during the Agranat Commission, which investigated the problems leading to Egypt and Syria's surprise attack on Israel 50 years earlier, seem to persist today. The quote above, about Unit 8200, indicates that the Israelis are still overly dependent upon high-grade positive confirmation of a threat – rather than structured analytic methods and a range of sources – to assess a threat with measured confidence. This dependence leaves advanced states vulnerable: if all you are looking for is positive proof, which is often an impossible task, you are bound to be surprised. Likewise, Israel's enemies understand its technological advantages. Why would they leave breadcrumbs there if not solely to deceive? This was as true in 1972–3 as it was in 2023.

There is also evidence of a new Israeli 'conception', or preconception. In 1973, the conception was an Israeli assumption or paradigm that if Egypt were to attack, it would seek to regain all territory lost in 1967. Israel's defence intelligence therefore concluded that since Egypt lacked the means to do this, it would not dare try. This caused Israeli analysts to discount evidence that Egypt was preparing an offensive.[6] More recently, Israelis had assumed that Hamas preferred to avoid direct confrontation and instead wished to deal with economic problems and its own administrative interests rather than risk its destruction. This notion had been fostered, it is now obvious, by Hamas's seemingly timid responses in the clashes between Israel and Palestinian Islamic Jihad over the previous two years. This thinking made Israeli decision-makers even more likely to discount contrary evidence.

Compounding this conception were Israeli political exigencies. Having pursued a carrot-and-stick strategy of deterrence and collaboration with Hamas, Israeli leaders believed they could continue to transfer finance to Hamas and that it would continue to behave as though it was anything other than a resistance movement. Israel's hard-line, right-wing government has been intent on cracking down on Palestinians in the West Bank while giving the settler movement a freer hand to expand, even violently. Any discussion about the removal of troops from Gaza fuelled this political self-interest. It made sense to keep this government's radical base happy in the West Bank – far more sense than believing you were being fooled by Hamas. The chief of AMAN nourished this conception: his briefings confirmed, despite evidence to the contrary, that warnings from Gaza were nothing to worry about compared to the security needs of the West Bank.

In the Israeli system, the head of RAD reports to the head of AMAN. This assessment is carried forward to both the defence minister, Yoav Gallant, and Prime Minister Netanyahu. The latter two have been political enemies since Netanyahu attempted to sack Gallant in March 2023. The week before 7 October, 'senior IDF and Defence Ministry personnel estimated…that Hamas is not interested in, or preparing for war'.[7] The thinking ran that Hamas would not risk the gains it had secured for Gazans during its indirect talks with Israel. Israel's national security adviser argued that Hamas was 'very, very restrained'. It is procedurally likely that the prime minister was at this meeting, or at least privy to the assessment briefing. That same week Netanyahu led a security meeting focused on Iran, not Hamas. These meetings sanctioned the transfer of Israeli troops away from Gaza.

When the warning finally arrived, it left only a few hours to respond, and still does not seem to have been taken seriously. *Haaretz* describes a meeting with the IDF and Shin Bet (Israel's internal security service, also known as *Sherut HaBitachon HaKlali*, or Shabak) the night before the surprise attack. They discussed warnings of a terrorist infiltration. They clearly did not appreciate the potential scale: they decided to deploy a few specialist counterterrorist units to the area, just in case. They did not redeploy troops from elsewhere or call reserves. Nobody in the security apparatus decided to inform the troops, recall soldiers on leave or inform border installations.[8] This decision, as it happens, led to disastrous losses for Israeli special forces, who should not substitute line infantry.

These are the facts as published at the time of writing. Besides the anec- dote above about late-notice warning, up until late December 2023 we heard barely a whisper about Shin Bet's role in the debacle. Then, Israel's Channel 12 reported that the security service had indeed been handling a human source within Hamas which, two months prior to 7 October, delivered accurate information about Hamas's plans, including the date of the attack. The source, codenamed *mavo'ah*, Hebrew for 'fountain', had passed on intelligence received from an insider. Shin Bet concluded that the information was 'not meaningful' – the source was relatively new and inexperienced, and their reliability was not yet clearly established. Shin Bet, like the army, is promising its own internal investigation.[9]

In this context, it is worth noting that Shin Bet, like Mossad, is a branch of the Prime Minister's Office (not the Interior and Foreign Ministries, as in other countries). We will only develop a clear understanding of what went wrong following an independent public investigation.

Anatomy of intelligence failure

Journalists and scholars have already pounced on some standard com- parisons for the failure of Israeli intelligence to 'connect the dots' of the warning signs.[10] This is a reference to the 9/11 Commission Report, which itself was addressing Roberta Wohlstetter's 1962 study of the intelligence failure leading to the attack on Pearl Harbor in 1941.[11] In that text, Wohlstetter describes the difficulty in discerning 'signals' from 'noise' in a vast pool of data. Richard Betts, perhaps reacting to the obvious impos- sibility of remediating such a problem, argued that failure was inevitable and the best decision would be to prepare contingencies.[12] Erik Dahl's

Yahya Sinwar, the Palestinian head of
Hamas in Gaza, Gaza City, April 2022.

book *Intelligence and Surprise Attack* attempts to harmonise a range of approaches towards intelligence failure and surprise attack. In it, Dahl offers a 'theory of preventative action' – intelligence must provide specific, tactical and actionable warning to a receptive audience.[13] This theory is useful: it helps us understand that, in the case of 7 October, there was clearly specific, tactical and actionable warning which was disregarded. Dahl's theory provides a reasonable answer to the counterfactual question: what could have been done? It is safe to say that in the current case there was enough specific, tactical and actionable warning evidence available to maintain a higher level of readiness. However, like Wohlstetter, Dahl demands too much of the intelligence services. Is it really intelligence failure when the audience for a briefing is not receptive? This is too convenient for the political leadership. When are they accountable, if not in this case?

In *Why Intelligence Fails*, Robert Jervis presents a model which does not require hindsight to reform the way intelligence is organised and created. Jervis describes two overarching categories. The first is that intelligence can be wrong (I am not convinced this should always be judged as failure, especially since our working definition permits error when professional standards are upheld). The second is about the process: how do we rate the analytic craft and its product? Have analysts examined the full range of evidence and alternative hypotheses? Have they used structured analytic techniques (SATs) to bring their conclusions away from intuition and towards something more social-scientific? Have staff attempted to wrestle with their biases, their language, and the consequences of getting it wrong?[14] This is a helpful model for both reformers of today and historians like me. Often, we try not to judge the past by contemporary standards but the standard of its own: this gives us a model for looking backwards at cases such as Pearl Harbor, when SATs did not exist. It also helps us diagnose contemporary issues such as the case of 7 October.

Recent scholarship on Israeli intelligence illuminates a few salient problems. Israeli intelligence generally eschews SATs and defence intelligence doctrine, suggesting that these limit creative thinking and constrain analysts.[15] They prefer an 'artistic' approach to analysis, 'underpinned by intuition, creativity, imagination and inductive reasoning. Instinct and experience are perceived as crucial skills. Inductive reasoning based on recognising patterns in past experiences...places more emphasis on tacit knowledge.'[16] Given the evidence available about warning failure, described above, the danger of these attitudes becomes apparent. For his PhD research on Israel's intelligence culture, Itai Shapira's interviewees from AMAN described its un-corporate culture. Their evidence reveals a systemic misunderstanding of SATs, doctrine and analytic craft. A system which emphasises intuition and inductive reasoning based on experience is bound to fall victim to 'WYSIATI' bias: 'What you see is all there is.' They would be prone to ignoring young women whose observations led to a different, and incidentally more accurate, analysis than the intuitions of their superior officers.

There is a misconception in the scholarship and some quarters of the profession, and clearly in Israel too, that SATs create conformity and falsely claim to eliminate certain biases. In fact, new research shows that although SATs are not useful for eliminating two specific types of bias, they are still valuable as a means to move analysts away from their fallible intuitions (incidentally, intuition-based reasoning is also a common problem in my own profession of history).[17] As a history instructor on a Master of Arts in Intelligence and Security Studies programme which teaches these methods, I must note here that watching our students use these techniques has changed my mind about them. I have seen how, by forcing analysts to challenge their way of thinking and to create an auditable record of their process, they learn to hold themselves to account for their product.

In short, the fundamental problems leading to intelligence failure in Israel may well have been both doctrinal and methodological. Warning from the *tatzpitaniot* or from a cell within 8200 needs to be worked into the analytic process and accounted for. That is, any analytic product which is going to discount such warnings needs to show the process of why: what competing hypotheses can be eliminated? What is the impact if we are right or wrong? What key assumptions about Hamas require re-examination, and on what schedule? In the absence of positive proof, what other indicators might support the minority view that Hamas was preparing an attack?

In addition to method, there seems to be an issue with process. Israel lacks an all-source intelligence analysis body comprised of its own professional analytic staff. It has nothing like the UK's Joint Intelligence Committee (JIC) or the American National Intelligence Council.[18] Shapira's Israeli interviewees largely rejected these ideas as well,

An Israeli airstrike in Gaza City on the day Hamas
launched its attack on Israel, 7 October 2023.

suggesting that these were foreign solutions which do not fit Israel's informal, 'bottom-up' culture. The evidence emerging since 7 October perhaps illustrates that this bottom-up culture exists in myth alone. Amos Gil'ad, former director of AMAN's research and analysis department, stood apart, arguing that a formal statutory structure to coordinate defence, security and foreign intelligence was needed. Most interviewees agreed that Israel had no intelligence 'community' as such – that with Shin Bet and Mossad reporting to the prime minister and AMAN a branch of the army, there was no impetus for a coordinating body. Perhaps it could not work, but the evidence available about how leaders were briefed before 7 October certainly suggests that the current system is not good enough. Who is responsible for warning intelligence from Gaza? From Lebanon? Iran? The answer is not obvious and leaves room for overlap, competition and waste. Moreover, this structureless process sets no expectations for how confidence in assessment, or the lack thereof, is communicated to decision-makers. It depends entirely on the relationship between AMAN's chief, the defence minister and the prime minster.

New evidence has emerged on what the 'devil's advocate' department of AMAN had to say before 7 October. This department is a legacy of the Agranat Commission, which reformed the system following the failures of 1973. The department produces assessments which are meant to highlight some of the SAT-like questions discussed above. It tends to focus on issues of methodology and philosophy, which RAD lacks.[19] Little is known about its process, although there is some research emerging which shows it has had a positive impact on decisions.[20] Yet this structure forces the analysis to take place at a very high level – it is left up to the chief of AMAN's own judgement (and that of his inner circle). This would be considered unusual, even unprofessional, in other Western settings. I don't think this is a good way to communicate confidence, or a lack thereof, in one's judgement.

In early 2024, a senior officer of AMAN discussed the problem with Channel 12. The officer, A, incidentally also a woman, reported that the devil's advocate department is not really a department, but a single officer. There are not typically serious discussions about this officer's work. They lack the resources to perform the kind of in-depth research undertaken by RAD. A stated that there are no other one-person departments. The chief of AMAN, Major General Aharon Haliva, was inclined to red-team issues, but, according to A, 'there was supposed to be a devil's advocate department. It is clear to everyone that these statements are lip-service.' The assessment was already determined by that stage – that a red-team exercise is pointless and unlikely to change minds. Indeed, A said that Haliva tends to resist opinions which go against his judgement. His staff, according to this one source, challenge him cautiously, and seemingly rarely. This problem of structure, process and personality manifested a week before 7 October. The heads of the devil's advocate department and RAD discussed with Haliva an assessment which contradicted his premise: that Hamas was interested in maintaining the quiet. Hamas, it was argued, needed to act against normalisation with Saudi Arabia and the post-2021 recovery of the Palestinian National Authority from its near collapse. The warning included the likelihood of shooting and kidnapping attempts, not an operation on the scale of 7 October. It is unclear whether it was informed by real-time access to the data produced by the female NCO known as V, in 8200 or by the border spotters. This view was widely disseminated, to no effect.[21] It would seem that the myth of a bottom-up, creative culture in Israeli intelligence persists; recent events should dispel the notion entirely.

When Israel convenes a commission of inquiry, one hopes that organisational design will be part of its remit, and likewise the issues of methodology and responsibility discussed above. We would naturally expect it to look at what evidence was available, and how and why it was missed. Or how and why, when positive warning arrived with hours to go, the response was so weak. However, above all, I would expect that the relationship with the political level would be scrutinised. The issue that continues to nag at me is the briefing in September which led to the withdrawal of IDF battalions to the West Bank from Gaza. What standard of evidence could have convinced the army that this was unadvisable? What about the politicians?

An air gap between intelligence collection agencies and decision-makers is essential. Analysis within each agency remains important, but an intermediary level must address major strategic insights, bridging the gap between intelligence services and political leadership. If true, it is shocking that senior AMAN officers did not have access to the whole pool of data. Similarly, assessments often bypass Mossad and Shin Bet data and remain confined within military boundaries, not reaching a national level. Even in recent reporting, we see that this structureless system encourages blame and makes accountability difficult to achieve. The Channel 12 piece on the devil's advocate department commented, 'in Haliva's defence', that the head of RAD is not subordinate to the chief of AMAN but is the national assessor of intelligence who disseminates his work to the entire political and military complex. It should be noted that Shapira's work shows this is in fact a dual role. Likewise, 'Shin Bet and Mossad see and analyse the same raw material and independently agreed that Hamas was deterred'.[22] This is perhaps the clearest sign of a broken process, and illustrates the need for a national assessment staff which draws upon all collection services and reports to a broader range of stakeholders at the political level. An Israeli-style JIC would be a cultural shift – Israel's founding prime minister David Ben-Gurion centralised control of Shin Bet and Mossad within the Prime Minister's Office to force rival ministers (especially his foreign minister) from these discussions. Nonetheless, reform is imperative. The current structure fails to serve its purpose if leaders cannot ask basic questions and receive reliable answers. The intelligence community must undergo a redesign, holding itself to high professional and social-scientific standards, challenging perspectives, maximising collaboration and detaching national assessment from the discrete interests of each agency and politicians.

Conclusion

Having looked at all these factors, it is worth returning to the question of intelligence failure. Did Israeli intelligence fail because disaster struck, or because it failed to warn? Did it fail to warn because it ignored good evidence and lacked a methodology, or because professional staff agreed that the risk from Hamas was low? Would changing the way these assessments took place, separating them from the politicians, have changed the outcome? It is hard to know, but this kind of counterfactual would be simple enough to wargame in order to reach a plausible answer. This sort of social-scientific approach to analysis ought to be embraced by Israel's intelligence services as they turn to some soul-searching. It will only be possible to answer these questions in full following an independent inquiry, with full access to the evidence.

The lessons we learn from this case should also help us develop clearer ideas about the phenomenon of failure. We see that there were competent staff who got it right but could not convince commanders or more senior staff. Although the evidence available remains limited, it is still safe to say that failure lay in a system which could not give these soldiers' perspectives a chance to have an impact. Despite what its members say, Israel does create an institutional assessment in the person of the senior leaders of RAD and AMAN – whatever persuades them becomes the army's point of view. This approach might work routinely, and even lead to excellent results, but it falls apart under the pressures of uncertainty, political tension and a structure which favours stovepipes over collaboration.

The definition of intelligence failure I have offered admittedly complicates the case for failure on 7 October. Since AMAN's professional standards are woolly, diffuse and variable, it may be impossible to measure a failure to meet them. Equally, it will be difficult to hold such a system accountable. This further highlights the importance for an investigation into the structures and processes which contributed to error and failure. Israel clearly needs an independent analytic body with access to all sources and which is able to answer any cabinet minister's request for information. Such a staff could view warning evidence without the baggage and biases of having produced it. They could track it without being distracted by the opinions of local generals or institutional pressures. This is especially important in a political landscape where senior and retired generals often lead successful political careers.

An Israeli-style JIC would create a national-level assessment for policymakers to consume, underpinned by professional analysts held to a consistent doctrine. Their product must be available to all stakeholders, not just two cabinet members. Analysts must be drawn away from their intuition in such a system, and forced to systematically challenge their grasp of a problem as evidence emerges and perspectives evolve. One would expect that such a system would remediate the current lack of accountability which prevails between the general staff and the cabinet. Israel needs an intelligence process which offers military and political leaders something useful, while holding them all accountable to their roles and for their responsibilities.

1. Agencies. Egypt intelligence official says Israel ignored repeated warnings of 'something big'. *Times of Israel*, 9 October 2023, https:www.timesofisrael.com/egypt-intelligence-official-says-israel-ignored-repeated-warnings-of-something-big/.
2. Katie Bo Lillis, Zachary Cohen, Alex Marquardt and Natasha Bertrand. US intelligence warned of the potential for violence days before Hamas attack. CNN, 13 october 2023, https:edition.cnn.com/2023/10/13/politics/us-intelligence-warnings-potential-gaza-clash-days-before-attack/index.html.
3. Yaniv Kubovich. The women soldiers who warned of a pending Hamas attack – and were ignored. *Haaretz*, 20 November 2023, https:www.haaretz.com/israel-news/2023-11-20/ty-article-magazine/.premium/the-women-soldiers-who-warned-of-a-pending-hamas-attack-and-were-ignored/0000018b-ed76-d4f0-affb-eff740150000.
4. Ronen Bergman and Adam Goldman. Israel knew Hamas's attack plan more than a year ago. *New York Times*, 2 December 2023, https:www.nytimes.com/2023/11/30/world/middleeast/israel-hamas-attack-intelligence.html.
5. Ben Caspit. Disclosure: the shelved report of 8200 on the negligence that led to the massacre in the South. *Maariv* [web edition], 24 February 2024, https:www.maariv.co.il/journalists/Article-1078519.
6. Itai Shapira. The Yom Kippur intelligence failure after fifty years: what lessons can be learned? *Intelligence and National Security*, vol 38, 2023, pp. 978–1002. 'Extensive research has been published about the failure of Israeli intelligence in the Yom Kippur War in 1973, mainly in the context of flawed analysis and strategic surprise. Fifty years after the war, the current article uses an intelligence studies lens to describe major lessons which can be learned from this failure of early warning. Such lessons include the required focus of strategic intelligence on identifying change rather than continuity, the need for explicit analytical methodology beyond inductive reasoning, the importance of integrating assessment of adversary intentions and capabilities, the risk of over-reliance on raw information, and the need for a culture encouraging contrarian thinking.'
7. Yaniv Kubovich and Jonathan Lis. Why Israel's defenses crumbled in face of Hamas' assault. *Haaretz*, 8 October 2023, https:www.haaretz.com/israel-news/2023-10-08/ty-article/.premium/six-significant-failures-that-lead-to-one-point-collapse-vs-hamas/0000018b-0f15-dfff-a7eb-afddobb80000.
8. Kubovich, The women soldiers.
9. Elana Dayan and Sarit Magen. Uvda exposé: warning which reached Shabak. *Keshet 12*, 27 December 2023, https:www.mako.co.il/news-military/6361323ddea5a810/Article-0a034bff26cac81026.htm [accessed 11 January 2024].
10. Bergman and Goldman, Israel knew Hamas's attack plan; Uri Bar-Joseph and Avner Cohen. How Israel's spies failed – and why escalation could be catastrophic, *Foreign Policy*, 19 October 2023, https:foreignpolicy.com/2023/10/19/israel-intelligence-gaza-nuclear-weapons-hezbollah-iran-escalation-could-be-catastrophic.

11. Roberta Wohlstetter. *Pearl Harbor: Warning and Decision.* Stanford, CA: Stanford University Press, 1962. 'The results at Pearl Harbor, were sudden, concentrated and dramatic. The failure, however, was cumulative, widespread and rather drearily familiar. This why surprise, when it happens to a government, cannot be described just in terms of startled people. Whether at Pearl Harbor or at the Berlin Wall, surprise is everything involved in a government (or in an alliance's) failure to anticipate effectively.'

12. Richard K Betts. Analysis, war, and decision: why intelligence failures are inevitable. *World Politics*, vol 31, no 1, 1978, pp. 61–89.

13. Erik J Dahl. *Intelligence and Surprise Attack: Failure and Success from Pearl Harbor to 9/11 and Beyond.* Washington DC: Georgetown University Press, 2013.

14. Robert Jervis. *Why Intelligence Fails: Lessons from the Iranian Revolution and the Iraq War* (Cornell Studies in Security Affairs). Ithaca, NY; London: Cornell University Press, 2010.

15. Itai Shapira. The Israeli idea of intelligence: anatomy of the Israeli national intelligence culture (unpublished thesis). University of Leicester, 2023, https:figshare.le.ac.uk/articles/thesis/The_Israeli_Idea_of_Intelligence_ Anatomy_of_the_Israeli_National_Intelligence_Culture/24204042/1 [accessed 13 November 2023], pp. 108, 217.

16. Ibid, p. 150.

17. Martha Whitesmith. *Cognitive Bias in Intelligence Analysis: Testing the Analysis of Competing Hypotheses Method.* Edinburgh: Edinburgh University Press, 2020.and proposes a more effective approachReveals that a key element of current training provided to the UK and US intelligence communities (and likely all 5-EYES and several European agencies

18. Shapira, The Israeli idea of intelligence, p. 101.

19. Ibid, p. 59.

20. Good research is emerging, though; see Eyal Pascovich, The devil's advocate in intelligence: the Israeli experience. *Intelligence and National Security*, vol 33, no 6, 2018, pp. 854–65.

21. Danny Hecht. Warning of the head of the devil's advocate department one week before the war. *N12*, 7 January 2024, https:www.mako.co.il/news-military/2024_q1/ Article-c07831ec3b0ec81027.htm.

22. Ibid.

INFORMATION, ASSESSMENT AND ACCOUNTABILITY

US army personnel secure an
industrial complex thought to have been
a site for WMD, Baquba, Iraq, 2003.

THE BUTLER REVIEW:
AN APPRAISAL 20 YEARS ON

Suzanne Raine

On 3 February 2004, Jack Straw, then British Secretary of State for Foreign and Commonwealth Affairs, announced in the House of Commons the establishment of a committee to review intelligence on weapons of mass destruction (WMD) in the run-up to the Iraq War of 2003.[1] There were to be only five members of the committee: it was led by former Cabinet secretary Robin Butler, Lord Butler of Brockwell; the other members were former Chief of the Defence Staff (CDS) Field Marshal the Lord Inge; Sir John Chilcot; Ann Taylor MP, Chair of the Intelligence and Security Committee (ISC); and Michael Mates MP (also on the ISC). The committee had access to all intelligence reports and other government papers and could interview and call witnesses. Working to a tight timescale, it met 36 times in five months and the completed review was published on 14 July 2004.

The review's purpose was to investigate intelligence coverage of WMD; to investigate the accuracy of intelligence on Iraqi WMD up to March 2003; to examine any discrepancies between the intelligence gathered, evaluated and used by government before the conflict and what has subsequently turned out to be the case; and to 'make recommendations to the Prime Minister for the future on the gathering, evaluation and use of intelligence on WMD, in light of the difficulties of operating in countries of concern'.[2] Given the subsequent absorption of the review's recommendations by the UK assessment machinery, it is worth noting how narrowly defined its purpose was at this stage.

The review is a succinct but rich document and, while it can at times seem dated, is still very relevant. It was written at a time before mass data, when the process of collection and analysis of intelligence relied less completely on technology. Paradoxically, although search tools were much more basic, the amount of material to be searched was smaller and the means of retrieval easier because records were more simply categorised and codified. As such, the review is perhaps one of the last close looks at intelligence and analysis in a time just preceding the big data age. It provides a perfect case study for how the threat of war becomes war; how initial judgements become assumptions and then become a baseline over time; how difficult it can be to look for a threat which may or may not be there; and how this is made more difficult when the threat actor wants to appear threatening in order to deter an attack.

Much of the immediate commentary focused on the following findings: that the intelligence used to make the case for the invasion of Iraq was flawed; that the Joint Intelligence Committee (JIC) should not have played such a public role in making the case; that the conclusions of the assessment had been distorted in order to persuade; and that the informal style of government consultation did not allow for sufficient challenge or the inclusion of all expertise.[3] There has been less focus externally on the process issues identified by Butler as the causes of this, or of the review's prescriptions for how this kind of failure might be prevented in the future. A contemporary exception would be Richard Aldrich's journal article from 2005, 'Whitehall and the Iraq War: the UK's four intelligence enquiries', which suggested that although the enquiries had been useful in understanding the nature of the intelligence failure, none dealt with the issue of the interaction between intelligence analysis and policymaking.[4]

Within government, immediate remedial action was taken through the Butler Implementations Group, led by the Security and Intelligence Coordinator, Sir David Omand.[5] This response to Butler's recommendations both in terms of *techniques* of collection, review and analysis, and in terms of *structure* (division of collection, analysis and policy) became quickly embedded to the point where the doctrine for the production, issuing, analysis and assessment of intelligence was reset, and the relationship between those doing the assessment and those making policy redefined. Over 20 years 'Butler' has become shorthand for an approach to intelligence collection and assessment in the UK government which stops short of being formally codified but whose elements are clear: validation of sources; separation of reporting chains within agencies; separation of assessment from policy; introduction of confidence statements; formalised challenge; professionalisation of analysis; and the JIC Chair to be beyond influence. Thus the response to the recommendations has defined the practice, possibly beyond anything the author of the review intended. In a section entitled 'Risks to good assessment', the review comments that: 'It is a well-known phenomenon within intelligence communities that the memory of past failures can cause over-estimation next time around.'[6]

This essay will look at six aspects of the recommendations to assess the degree of implementation 20 years on, and consider whether some remedies for past failures might also be limiting intelligence assessment today.

Validation of sources

The Review focused on how sources had been validated. It noted 'weaknesses in the effective application by SIS [the Secret Intelligence Service] of its validation procedures'.[7] Actions taken in response fundamentally changed the way sources were validated. As the review observed, intelligence 'operates in a field of particular difficulty. By definition the data it is trying to provide have been deliberately concealed.'[8] Human intelligence is usually only second-hand at best, mediated through a case officer, and more likely to be third- or fourth-hand. The collection of intelligence on weapons of mass destruction in Iraq was particularly difficult because the subject matter was so technical, and the information so closely guarded. There was a risk of misunderstanding, especially if there were multiple languages involved, and pressure on both the agent providing the reporting and the case officer to be sufficiently expert to make sense of it and test it. It needed to be clear whether the informant had been properly quoted, all the way along the chain, and whether the access they claimed to the information was credible. Even a long-term trusted source could pass on poor information with the best of intentions, for example if they did not know their sub-source well enough. Add in the question of motivation – to mislead, persuade, profit – and the challenge increases. It is important to discern whether the informant has other agendas, or is primarily motivated financially (in which case it might be expected that the incentive is to provide information they know intelligence agencies will be prepared to pay for).

The review stated:

> One reason for the number of agents whose reports turned out to be unreliable or even questionable may be the length of the reporting chains…Another reason may be that agents who were known to be

reliable were asked to report on issues going beyond their usual territory…A third reason may be that, because of the scarcity of sources and the urgent requirement for intelligence, more credence was given to untried agents than would normally be the case.[9]

This focus on authority, reliability and the sourcing chain offered a welcome clarity. Any report could only ever be as good as the weakest link in the chain. The expectation was clear:

> Our review has shown the vital importance of effective scrutiny and validation of human intelligence sources and of their reporting to the preparation of accurate JIC assessments and high-quality advice to ministers. We urge the Chief of SIS to ensure that this task is properly resourced and organised to achieve that result.[10]

Action was taken. On 20 July 2004, Prime Minister Tony Blair told Parliament that four things would happen in response to Butler's recommendations: the immediate appointment of a new JIC Chair, the conversion of the informal group into a Cabinet committee, the separation of the JIC assessments and policy and, critically, that 'SIS has appointed a senior officer to work through the findings and recommendations of the Butler Review, who will focus on the resourcing and organisation of the SIS's validation process'.[11]

This had a long-term effect: it imposed a discipline and rigour on the process of validating, and passed on a much greater level of transparency about the confidence in the sourcing to the intelligence analysts through a system which graded individual reports at high, medium and low confidence. As technical capabilities developed, it became theoretically possible to devote an ever-greater resource to understanding where the intelligence had come from and whether it was likely to be correct. But validating a long sourcing chain in repressive or dangerous circumstances can be almost impossibly difficult and prohibitively time-consuming. Even though it might in theory be possible positively to identify the sub-source or sub-sub-source, then to check that they have access to speak authoritatively and to understand and validate their motives, in practice the cost and effort necessary is often disproportionate in terms of time and risk, particularly to the sources themselves. This calculation is compressed when a report is time-sensitive and potentially high-impact

Lord Butler and Foreign Affairs Committee
member Ann Taylor, London, 2004.

– there simply may not be time to do the validation necessary. The bar for 'high-confidence' reporting is high; criteria could not be relaxed without accepting a greater level of imprecision. Therefore, while the validation process is consistently and thoroughly applied, it is frequently impossible to have high confidence in the entirety of the chain. The end result is that much reporting has to be issued at 'low confidence'.

This absolutely legitimate requirement for thoroughness passes the burden of testing the intelligence on to the analysts. It raises complex issues about how to treat low-confidence reporting in assessment, particularly where the reporting is politically or time-sensitive or contains a threat. It is not necessarily a given that low-confidence reporting is any less accurate than high-confidence reporting; the confidence descriptor communicates, rather, that it is not possible to be sure. In addition, the validation system means it is almost impossible to avoid discriminating against reporting from new or untested sources: a new source would almost always be issued at low confidence, but could provide critical information about a threat, for example. This passes the responsibility to the analyst to work out whether to take it seriously. An assessment that a threat is imminent, based on low-confidence reporting, is difficult to communicate.

The review notably has only one reference to GCHQ, so even by the standards of the day it does not address the separate question about whether reports produced through technical means are also not vulnerable to validation issues. Richard Aldrich rightly suggested that this was an extraordinary omission, given that there must have also been signals intelligence relevant to the WMD question.[12] It could be argued that the lack of emphasis in the review on limitations and vulnerabilities of reporting derived from technical means has left the assessment community with fewer inherited guidelines, particularly in an era of artificial intelligence, where the quality of the question asked can have a vast impact on the answer produced.

Structures for issuing intelligence reports
The review observed that processes within the SIS were not conducive to validation because the requirements and production officers reported to the same line manager.[13] It made a number of detailed comments about the internal structures, recommending that the validation process must

include a separate auditing element and that validation must not suffer owing to urgency for information, pressure to produce and limitations of resources.[14] These structural issues were swiftly addressed;[15] there is now absolute separation in management terms between production and requirements up to director-general level, mitigating to some extent the possibility that pressure might be put on junior reports officers to issue reporting which has not been properly validated or quantified. No structural solution is perfect, however; the review's suggestion creates two lines of activity, something which has the potential for tension when one line of activity is seen to be obstructing or holding up the other. This will continue to need active management.

Division between assessment and policymaking.
While the review is clear about the need to separate production from issuing of reporting, it is less explicit about how assessment and policy should be kept separate throughout the process, noting that senior policy roles are members of the JIC. Aldrich, in his near-contemporary response, noted that the review 'was carefully steered away from issues of how intelligence connected with high level decisions',[16] and it is indeed on this question that the recommendations are most vague. The review states that:

> the assessment process must be informed by an understanding of policy-makers' requirements for information, but must avoid being so captured by policy objectives that it reports the world as policy-makers would wish it to be rather than as it is. The JIC is part (and an important part) of the UK's governmental machinery or it is nothing; but to have any value its product must be objective.[17]

The recommendations called for 'clearer and more effective dividing lines between assessment and advocacy', having examined whether 'analysis or assessment appears to have been coloured by departmental policy or other agendas'.[18] Although the review found no evidence that assessments had been influenced by the policy positions of departments, it stressed that policy imperatives must not dominate objective assessment. Given that it was vague on how exactly this was to be implemented, it is interesting to observe how seriously this injunction was taken, how it has been interpreted, and the long-term effect it has had on the relationship between intelligence assessment and high-level decisions.

Twenty years on, the understanding that Butler proscribes policy influence on analytical judgements has entrenched a doctrinal separation of policy and analysis. Although the core membership of the JIC has not changed, including a number of senior policymaking officials, there is now a severe structural division between assessment and policymaking at every level of the process below the JIC. There is a division within the agencies between requirements and production, and the process of producing a JIC paper involves analysts and reports officers rather than policy officials. This has a clear, intended consequence: it enables professional assessment and analysis staff – who speak as authoritative and independent voices in policy meetings (to be beyond influence) – to lead on the process of producing the assessment, and it preserves the position of analysis and assessment as secure from political influence.

There is, however, an unintended consequence: this professional division limits the use that government makes of its analytical capability. Since analysis and assessment staff are not considered to be included as a part of policymaking, the UK government does not use its own assessment community to test its policy options. While the United States, for example, engages its assessment community in policy options analysis when formulating policy, the UK does not. In practice, this means that when policymaking officials consider different approaches to a particular foreign policy challenge or adversary, they do so without analysis of the likely impact of these options on the adversary, except that provided by those writing the policy. Butler does not expressly prohibit this, but it has been taken to be a natural consequence of the position that policy and analysis should not mix.

While it remains an absolute that analysis and assessment should be objective and independent, and policymaking should be a separate process, this does mean there is no part of the process where the rigorous thinking and analytical techniques of the professional analysis and assessment capability are applied to the possible futures conjured up by policy choices. The doctrinal separation of analysis of an adversary's actions from analysis of the effect of possible policy choices (including their effect on the adversary) means it is not possible to produce a piece of objective and independent assessment that considers what might be the outcome of actions x or y. Policy options analysis is core business for the US and other

UK allies, and it ought to be possible for the UK to do this without contravening Butler's recommendations. The circumstances now are very different, not least because the recommendations on professionalising analysis have been implemented.

Professionalisation of the analysis and assessment community
One of the most straightforward recommendations was that the Security and Intelligence Coordinator should consider 'whether there should be a specialism of analysis with a career structure and room for advancement, allowing the Assessments Staff to include some career members'.[19] This has, at least in part, been achieved. There is now a director-level post of Professional Head of Intelligence Analysis (PHIA) in the Joint Intelligence Organisation (JIO), and the role of intelligence analyst is one of the 19 civil service professions offering a career structure, with room for advancement and training.[20] An assessment academy has been created where analysts across government departments have the same instruction in analytical techniques and processes. Tradecraft which addresses risks of groupthink and how to challenge 'prevailing wisdom' has been thoroughly embedded in training and doctrine.

The review's second criticism was that the resources given to analysis and assessment were not sufficient to meet the needs of effective policymaking:

> The cost of the Assessments Staff is minimal in relation to the amounts the nation spends on the collection of intelligence. It is a false economy to skimp on the machinery through which expensively collected intelligence passes to decision makers. We recommend that the Security and Intelligence Coordinator reviews the size of the Assessments Staff, and in particular considers whether they have available the volume and range of resources to ask the questions which need to be asked in fully assessing intelligence reports and in thinking radically.[21]

Twenty years on, the questions of how analysis and assessment are resourced and whether they are sufficiently resourced remain to be addressed, and there is no indication of the political will to do so. In part this problem arises because there is no department whose dominant function is to perform analysis. Since the government funding process requires departments to bid competitively to the Treasury, the effect is repeatedly to fail to make a persuasive and coherent case for a significant increase in analytical capability.[22]

The question of whether analysts are in a position to think 'radically' is a separate one, which is tied to issues about confidence, uncertainty, imagination and risk. It may be, ironically, that Butler's recommendations reduce the room for analysts to think radically if, at the same time, they are required always to be right.

Communicating uncertainty

A key issue was the place of uncertainty in assessment. The review asked 'whether JIC assessments are drafted and presented in a way which best helps readers to pick up the range of uncertainty attaching to intelligence assessments'.[23]

The question of how to communicate uncertainty lies at the heart of the discipline of intelligence analysis and assessment, alongside the question of how assessment can draw a useful conclusion despite inevitable uncertainty. It might not be helpful, for example, for readers to 'pick up the range of uncertainty' if decisive action is needed. Over 20 years the response of the UK assessment community, facilitated by the appointment of the PHIA, has been to standardise the use of probabilistic language. Since much of the doctrine had been developed and honed within the Defence Intelligence Staff (DIS),[24] much of the practice adopted by the wider assessment community has its roots in the Ministry of Defence. Of particular note is the widespread adoption of the 'Probability Yardstick', which describes a scale of probabilities split into seven distinct numerical ranges, with terms assigned to each probability range.[25] It has become a common baseline for assessments across the UK government, and the language within it is found not only in products produced by Defence Intelligence (DI) and the JIO, but also in threat assessments produced by the Joint Terrorism Analysis Centre, among other specialised analytical bodies.[26]

The immediate (and positive) effect is to create a common language shared between analysts, but it is important to note that there are limitations which can become risks, as with any means by which uncertainty is described. The first is that it provides a quasi-scientific clarity which appeals to those who think numerically but which raises the potential for misunderstanding, not least because it obscures the uncertainty. The percentages of the Yardstick are simply a means by which the analyst communicates their degree of confidence in their own assessment. While it might be useful for decision-makers to have an impression of that degree of confidence, a decision will hang on the balance of probabilities (whether something is more likely than not), so the biggest calls are at the point of least certainty (the 50% mark).

The second inhibitor to the communication of uncertainty is that some of the language in the Probability Yardstick can be confusing. For example, the phrase 'it is a realistic possibility that a terrorist group brought down that plane' actually communicates that it is more likely that a terrorist group did not bring down that plane (a less than 50% probability). Similarly, a conclusion that a blast was 'likely' caused by a missile only means that the analyst thinks this has tipped over the point of least certainty (50%), so the balance of probability is that it was a missile. When, for example, assessment is used to provide an attribution for an attack of whatever kind, 55–75% is not enough to provide a clear basis for action.

The 'Key Judgements' of JIC papers are an acute example of requirement for clear communication of uncertainty. They sit at the front of a JIC paper and provide a top-line summary of the conclusions. The review recommends that, where there are significant limitations in the intelligence, the JIC should state these clearly alongside the Key Judgements. This has led to the introduction of confidence statements ('low', 'medium' and 'high') in the JIC papers, which relate to the analytical confidence in the judgements, in addition to references throughout the paper to the intelligence base, which would also be described in terms of low, medium and high confidence. As Butler states: 'We conclude it is a serious weakness that the JIC's warnings on the limitations of intelligence underlying its judgements were not made sufficiently clear.'[27]

This builds in a difficult dynamic. If the purpose of the Key Judgements is to communicate clearly the analysis, and to do so with an equal force each time, then the judgements should be made independently of the confidence in the reporting and should not be undermined with a caveat about the analysts' own confidence in their judgement. The provision of confidence levels implicitly invites the reader to conduct their own additional amateur analysis on the judgements. For example, if a significant judgement is made with low confidence, or rests on a base of low-confidence reporting, it is unavoidable that this will undermine the weight of the judgement. A low-confidence judgement needs to have the same authority as a high-confidence judgement if the policymaker is to take decisions based on it, although the policymaker also needs to understand that one carries a greater level of risk. One solution would be to keep the confidence in the sourcing in the text, but to ensure that the Key Judgements result from analytical discipline which weighs the balance of probabilities to provide clear judgements, not ones that are ambiguous or re-interpretable.

Most importantly, it must be possible to make a bold judgement which is not underpinned by overwhelming reporting, otherwise the highest-confidence reports would be those where there was sufficient information to produce a state of near certainty, and the lowest confidence when the insights were fewest. This would preclude and/or undermine many cases where the analyst was required to provide a warning about an escalating area of concern where the lack of insight and intelligence was either a contributing factor to the concern or not relevant. As stated earlier when referring to validation of sources, it would be difficult to avoid a low-confidence judgement based on intelligence from a new source which had not been validated, but this might well contain information about a threat that needed to be taken seriously and acted on immediately.

When it comes to the question of the JIC providing a warning function, the analytical judgement therefore must be separated from the limitations of the sourcing of the information if it is to provide an effective warning, since heavily caveated warnings will not be heeded. It is notable that it is possible to do this in those analytical bodies which operate UK national threat levels, for example in the Joint Terrorism Analysis Centre, which does so for international terrorism.

Butler himself warned that the fear of making mistakes might encourage risk aversion. If the objective of the JIC meeting is to cohere and converge, then it is likely that the judgements for which there is less evidence will be whittled out. Despite the stated intention to increase challenge and avoid groupthink, the requirement for assessment to be backed up with validated reporting can make challenge more difficult, and this increases the risk that JIC papers arrive at lowest common denominator conclusions. 'Problems can arise if the JIC has to make bricks without (enough) straw,' said the review.[28]

The question remains how successfully to challenge a perceived wisdom if the challenge cannot be substantiated by better evidence than that backing up perceived wisdom. Butler highlights the obvious shortcomings of complementary reporting, but it is still difficult to argue against a weight of complementary reports if the contrary voice is relying on a single and untested source. Challenges based upon subject matter knowledge and previous experience are an important check on a drift towards a hardening orthodoxy, but they too have obvious limitations. In these circumstances, it is difficult to reconcile the requirement for a properly audited and footnoted assessment with the injunction to think radically. At its heart is a question of brave analysis: a timely and bold judgement can significantly alter the usefulness of the report and – if it is right – enable the government to get ahead of a problem. By definition the bold judgement will be the most risky, so the integrity of the analytical process needs to be clear.

Presenting intelligence judgements to the general public

The review noted the challenge of presenting intelligence judgements effectively to the general public, and concluded that in translating JIC judgements into the dossier, 'warnings were lost about the limited intelligence base on which some aspects of these assessments were being made'.[29] The question of what information should be published, by whom and in what format, continues to be a live one, most recently resurfacing with the decision to publicise intelligence assessments of Russian intentions before the invasion of Ukraine and to provide a DI daily update on social media after it had begun.[30] The arguments for doing so are unchanged, as Butler noted: 'We understand why the government felt it had to meet the mounting public and Parliamentary demand for information.'[31] Both before and after the Russian invasion of Ukraine, the UK government attempted to tell the general public what was known (while protecting sources) and at the same time convey the nuances of how difficult it is to know anything. Butler said: 'We conclude that, if intelligence is to be used more widely by governments in public debate in future, those doing so must be careful to explain its uses and limitations. It will be essential, too, that clearer and more effective dividing lines between assessment and advocacy are established when doing so.'[32] It could be argued that the managed release of intelligence assessments of

Russia's intentions before the invasion of Ukraine, and the DI daily updates, are a clear demonstration that the recommendations in Butler are still being taken seriously. In an interview with the *The Economist*, the outgoing JIC Chair, Simon Gass, took care to stress that this was the case.[33]

It is possible to conclude, therefore, that in all six of these areas, the recommendations in the Butler Review were taken seriously 20 years ago, and the bad practices and pitfalls it warns of then continue actively to be considered and guarded against today. These protective practices have enabled the professionalisation of intelligence assessment and analysis, and ensured rigour and discipline in the process. They have, however, had unintended consequences which can inhibit bold and radical judgements, obfuscate the clarity of warnings, and underuse the UK government's analytical capability when formulating policy. They may also pass on to policymakers the very uncertainty which the assessment is there to filter.

1. *Review of Intelligence on Weapons of Mass Destruction* (Butler Report), Session 2003–4, HC 898, p. 1, Our terms of reference.
2. Ibid.
3. See for example the summary of media top lines at: It reveals a litany of self-delusion. *Guardian*, 16 July 2004, https:www.theguardian.com/politics/2004/jul/16/iraq.butler1.
4. Richard J Aldrich. Whitehall and the Iraq War: the UK's four intelligence enquiries. *Irish Studies in International Affairs*, vol 16, 2005, pp. 73–88.
5. This group submitted a report to ministers on 10 March 2005 with recommendations 'on the implementation of all the conclusions of the Butler Review which require action'. See Cm.6492, *Review of Intelligence on Weapons of Mass Destruction: Implementation of its Conclusions*, 2005.
6. *Review of Intelligence*, p. 15, para 53.
7. Ibid, p. 109, para 444. Author's insertion.
8. Ibid, p. 9, para 27.
9. Ibid, p. 108, paras 440–2.
10. Ibid, p. 109, para 445.
11. Tony Blair, HC Deb. Iraq: volume 424: debated 20 July 2004. *Hansard*, https:hansard.parliament.uk/Commons/2004-07-20/debates/a2f5a062-33c2-4f96-930d-e1eac07898f3/Iraq.
12. Aldrich, Whitehall and the Iraq War.
13. *Review of Intelligence*, pp. 102–3, paras 413–23.
14. *Review of Intelligence*, p. 109, paras 444–5.
15. See Cm.6492, *Review of Intelligence on Weapons of Mass Destruction: Implementation of its Conclusions*.
16. Aldrich, Whitehall and the Iraq War.
17. *Review of Intelligence*, p. 16, para 58.
18. Dividing lines, ibid p. 115, para 468; on other agendas, ibid, p. 109, para 446.
19. *Review of Intelligence*, p. 145, para 600.
20. See https:www.civil-service-careers.gov.uk/professions/.
21. *Review of Intelligence*, p. 145, para 600.
22. Richard Aldrich made this case forcefully in 2005, and yet the assessment staff in the Cabinet Office remain small in contrast to the scale of the collection and policymaking efforts: Aldrich, Whitehall and the Iraq War.
23. *Review of Intelligence*, p. 145, para 602.
24. This name was shortened to Defence Intelligence (DI) in 2009.
25. The Probability Yardstick is explained on a number of UK government websites; see in particular Ministry of Defence, Defence Intelligence: communicating probability, https:www.gov.uk/government/news/defence-intelligence-communicating-probability. See also Philip H J Davies, The Defence Intelligence 'Daily Update' in this volume.

26. This list of analytical bodies is not exhaustive but illustrative. The probabilistic language is now common across government. Since the decision in 2022 to publish DI daily updates on the Russian invasion of Ukraine, this language – including its limitations – has become much more widely understood by academics and commentators. See for instance Philip H J Davies' contribution to this collection.

27. *Review of Intelligence*, p. 114, para 464.

28. Ibid, pp. 13–14, para 46.

29. Ibid, p. 76, para 311; ibid, p. 114, para 464.

30. See Huw Dylan, How has public intelligence transformed the way this war has been reported?, King's College London, 1 March 2022, https:www.kcl.ac.uk/how-has-public-intelligence-transformed-the-way-this-war-has-been-reported.

31. *Review of Intelligence*, p. 114, para 466.

32. Ibid, p. 114.

33. The boss of Britain's spies speaks. *The Economist*, 29 June 2023, https:www.economist.com/britain/2023/06/29/the-boss-of-britains-spies-speaks.

The latest Defence Intelligence Update
on the situation in Ukraine, 5 July 2022.

THE DEFENCE INTELLIGENCE 'DAILY UPDATE': CURRENT INTELLIGENCE AS PUBLIC SERVICE ANNOUNCEMENT

Philip H J Davies

Since the outbreak of the Russia–Ukraine war the UK's defence intelligence organisation, somewhat unhelpfully branded Defence Intelligence (DI), has been turning out a daily briefing, the Intelligence Update, on Twitter (now X). The Update has received considerable press attention and has even become the basis of a near-daily article in London's *Evening Standard* newspaper. Reactions have been varied, from cynical dismissal of yet another information and influence operation by His Majesty's Government, through technical dissatisfaction with the analytical quality of the Update, to breathless enthusiasm for yet another British leap forward in transparency and open government. For the most part, however, the comments on and opinions of the Update have been based on a misperception of what *kind* of intelligence the Update is supposed to be, and the kinds of professional intelligence conventions on which it draws. While there may be concerns to raise about the Update, these are of a different order and deal with issues specific to analytic practice within DI. In particular, there appears to be a problem stemming from the intended refinements and improvements – in what Douglas MacEachin has termed 'analytic tradecraft' – that were initiated as a result of the furore about intelligence analysis after the 2003 invasion of Iraq.[1]

The Update's reception has ranged from fulsome enthusiasm to cynical doubt, and even dismay. On the fulsome side, Karla Adam of the *Washington Post* captures many of the favourable views that have been expressed. Adam locates the Update within a wider programme of disclosure and declassification underpinned by the ongoing impact of open government and increased transparency over the public-facing role and status of the intelligence community. In this context, the Update appears as part and parcel of the strategy of issuing public warning appreciations of the imminent Russian invasion that famously employed open-source satellite imagery, 'pre-bunking' Russian false flag operations and warnings of planned Russian irregular warfare actions that were not sourced but attributed, with evasive vagueness, to 'intelligence'. Noting that 'nowadays officials [in the UK] share declassified secrets in briefings with reporters', Adam adds that taking such information 'to a mass audience is a novel approach'. But doing so 'is not without risks', because 'sources or methods used to acquire intelligence could be exposed'. Consequently, 'the intelligence tweets are…still on the cautious side, and sanitized'. With such trade-offs in mind, the updates may be 'just the tip of the iceberg and sometimes detail what's available on other open-source outlets', but they offer 'a constant feed of tactical information'.[2]

By contrast, Jeffrey Michaels at the Royal United Services Institute (RUSI) argues: 'Not only is the intelligence void of useful facts and insightful judgements, the style and attention to detail leave much to be desired as well.' At some points, he adds, 'the updates reflect views that are so obvious one cannot help wondering how this constitutes "intelligence"', singling out the 1 March 2022 entry for stating that the use of artillery in densely populated urban areas 'greatly, increases the risk of civilian casualties'. Like Adam, Michaels notes the duplication between the Update and the information in the public domain on which it reports, but where Adam treats that as a minor caveat, Michaels complains that 'most of what is reported in the DI updates will already have appeared in the mainstream media and on social media, sometimes days beforehand'. Where Adam locates the Update in the wider context of intelligence disclosure and declassification, Michaels positions it as organisational politics. The daily updates are not, he argues, a declassified or unclassified product,[3] but 'the intelligence equivalent of a media event', which are significant because 'they derive from an intelligence organisation'. Their main purpose is not one of public information, nor even 'promoting a pro-Ukraine narrative', but instead 'putting DI and the MoD in the spotlight'.[4]

Above and beyond the weak analysis, poor presentation and institutional self-serving bias of the Update, Michaels is unhappy with its substantive focus. Slightly inconsistently with his 'not promoting a pro-Ukraine narrative' comment, he also complains that the analysis is 'too one-sided, as it looks almost exclusively at Russian actions and avoids any substantive examination of the Ukrainian side'. The failure to assess both

sides is a chronic deficiency of intelligence, because 'intelligence organisations have a tendency to focus on Red (enemy forces) rather than Blue
(friendly forces)'. 'In other words,' he continues, 'despite the ostensibly
self-evident need for a holistic understanding of the war, there tends to be
little desire to analyse the strengths, weaknesses and intentions of one's
allies.' The putative motivation, he suggests, is 'fear of embarrassment if
negative analyses are leaked'.[5]

The failure to assess friendly forces is something of a misrepresentation
of the intelligence problem, and is a line of argument worth scotching
sooner rather than later in this discussion. There is, of course, an established analytical methodology for assessing the relative weight of two belligerents, commonly referred to as 'correlation of forces', some examples
of which are available in the public domain.[6] This is generally easiest
when one is not closely invested in one side of the conflict; otherwise,
this shifts problems into a chronically troubled area known as 'net
assessment, that is, assessing one's own forces as against an adversary.
Net assessment is intrinsically problematic because, in principle, one's
own forces are not supposed to be the target of collection and assessment, ie of intelligence activity. It is also common to extend that proviso
to friendly forces, especially those of close allies. The eventual United
States solution to the problem was to move net assessment up and out of
the intelligence community as such to the National Security Council,
while in recent years in the UK net assessment sits outside and above DI
and within the office of the Secretary of State for Defence.[7] In a military
command staff, the correlation of hostile and friendly forces is handled
by the operations and planning cells, not the intelligence cell.[8]

The fundamental problem with both these commentaries about the
DI Update is that they rest upon perceptions and expectations modelled
on national intelligence institutions, processes and products rather than
an understanding of military and defence intelligence. In an especially
peculiar irony, the misunderstanding of the Update's significance, aims
and actual quality are a product of the revolution in government transparency about intelligence that has swept the democratic world in the
decades since the Church Committee of the 1970s, the American Senate
Select Committee to Study Governmental Operations with Respect to
Intelligence Activities.[9] The political classes in the West in the 21st century have an unprecedented public awareness and understanding of
national intelligence driven by the successive scandals, failures and

post-mortems that have prompted the creation of increasingly systematic and comprehensive architectures of intelligence oversight, accountability and scrutiny. As a result, public expectations of intelligence analysis and assessment, such as those expressed by Michaels and Adam, have been shaped by the lustration of national processes and assessment institutions, in the UK most prominently the Joint Intelligence Committee (JIC) and its supporting Joint Intelligence Organisation.[10]

By comparison, defence and military intelligence entities and their work are – again ironically – appreciably less well understood in civil society, even though they have always been less secretive. To a degree, the role and issues of defence and military intelligence affairs have tended to be drowned out by the level of public attention given to national intelligence functions and organisations, and the volume of information about them and their work that has come into the public domain. But it also has to be said that the term 'intelligence' in the civilian and military realms means very different things. As I have argued elsewhere, civilians tend to see this intelligence in terms of espionage and the exploitation of covertly acquired information in synthesis with less secret and open-source information, while the military has long treated it as an all-source, knowledge-management and analytic function resting primarily on open sources such as cartography, hydrology, non-English-language publications and what amounts to human geography.[11] Consequently, national intelligence on the one hand and defence and military intelligence on the other exist in two different worlds and perform two different tasks for two equally different sorts of purpose.

There are, therefore, two key items of context that need to be understood when trying to evaluate the DI Daily Update. The first is that it is produced by DI itself and therefore reflects defence and military intelligence conventions rather than national intelligence practices. The second is that the Update is a very specific type of intelligence product: *current intelligence*. Current intelligence is a fundamentally different analytic product from the kind of strategic assessments produced by the JIC or the US National Intelligence Council. These 'high powered reports for high powered people', as Michael Herman, former secretary of the JIC, once put it,[12] are more likely to be concerned with big-picture strategic issues and the sort of long-term forecasts the US intelligence community refers to as 'estimative intelligence'.[13] Indeed, one of the consequences of public perception based on JIC assessments is precisely the tendency to conflate *analysis* with *assessment*. As Lord Butler observed in 2004, analysis entails examining intelligence information 'in its own right'. This may be because it is necessary to 'convert complex technical evidence into descriptions of real-world objects or events'. Alternatively, the raw intelligence data might be 'scattered' across multiple lines of reporting, in which case analysis 'assembles individual intelligence reports into meaningful strands' to form a coherent picture.[14] Analysis asks, essentially, what the intelligence *means*. According to the Cabinet Office Professional Head of Intelligence Assessment, however, assessment is concerned with the 'so what?' of the available intelligence.[15] It seeks to fit the intelligence into bigger patterns, testing the sum total of the available reporting against alternative 'models' (ie hypotheses) to 'produce a picture which is more than the simple sum of the parts'.[16] Assessment, therefore, asks what that intelligence *implies*.

Current intelligence is typically more a matter of analysis rather than assessment. As its name suggests, it is concerned with much more mundane affairs of immediate concern and fine detail than assessment. The current UK joint intelligence doctrine defines current intelligence as 'intelligence that reflects the present situation at strategic, operational and/or tactical levels', which 'reflects a moment in time' and is therefore 'perishable' in terms of accuracy and relevance as events develop.[17] According to US intelligence community guidance, current intelligence seeks to 'apprise consumers of new developments and their background, to assess their significance, to warn of near term consequences, and to signal potentially dangerous situations in the near future'.[18] Indeed, there is a close, even integral, relationship between current intelligence and warning intelligence, to such a degree that the functions are often either combined or collocated.[19] By way of illustration, it was photographic current intelligence from U-2 re-connaissance flights that detected the offensive ballistic missiles in Cuba that a National Intelligence Estimate of 19 September 1962 had dismissed as a likelihood.[20] Likewise, it was current intelligence, mainly from communications intercepts, which detected the imminent April 1982 Argentine invasion of the Falklands that JIC assessments had concluded was unlikely any time before the autumn.[21] If intelligence is largely about asking 'what's going on?' and 'what's going to happen next?' (and occasionally 'what just happened?'), current intelligence is intended to answer the first of these.

In 1949, the well-respected Central Intelligence Agency (CIA) analyst

Sherman Kent deliberated in depth on the need for, and consequent nature of, current intelligence. Kent argued that current intelligence captures the target at a moment in time, 'stopping the clock' on entities and events which are in motion and evolving.[22] The basic role of current intelligence is to update the intelligence picture and report on change and the direction of change, with Kent noting: 'For example, it is as important to know that the standing military establishment of a potential enemy power is being demobilized as it is to know that it is being built up or merely reoriented around a new weapon or a new tactical concept.'[23] Change can follow many different alternative directions, and current intelligence needs to be alert to that. The question, Kent acknowledged, quickly becomes one of selecting what areas of activity and change need to be monitored and updated. There is, he noted, 'no categorical answer', but emphasis should be on matters 'positively germane' to policy and rank-ordered by relative importance.[24] Tasking, requirements and priorities are, therefore, at the heart of current intelligence.[25]

Current intelligence has, however, some crucial and often noted limitations. Political scientist and former CIA officer Stephen Marrin has warned that, compared with estimative, warning and in-depth 'research' intelligence, current intelligence production is 'the least analytical'. The immediate significance and limited shelf life of current intelligence means that 'time constraints do not permit analytic tradecraft to be applied', with 'tight deadlines' that often compel analysts to 'use short-cuts' and rely 'more on informed intuition than structured or rigorous methods'.[26] *Furthermore:*

> When the CIA emphasizes intelligence 'on demand' analysts meet the much shorter deadlines by reducing the scale and scope of their research as well as sidestepping the more laborious procedures by not rigorously scrutinizing assumptions or comparing working hypotheses to competing explanations. Many times current intelligence analysis consists of a single hypothesis – derived within the first hour of tasking – that the analyst intuitively believes is the best explanation for the data.[27]

The resulting 'frenetic pace' can produce an analytical 'drinking from a firehose' of information that may have 'eroded analysts' ability to acquire expertise'.[28] And this erosion inevitably means that any such analysis rests on a less developed and less well-informed understanding of the context and significance of the breaking intelligence news being reported.

A little like Adam and Michaels, Marrin's concerns about analytic rigour also apply national intelligence concerns and criteria of *assessment* to an *analytical* function that is largely, as Kent termed it, 'reportorial' and therefore minimally analytical and mainly factual in interest and content. However, one can also see in Marrin's description how the risks attendant on current intelligence are inherent limitations arising from the nature and timelines of such intelligence and its requirements. In this sense, those limitations are not so much foibles or failings as rationally calculated trade-offs by current intelligence analysts and their managers.

Despite the analytical and assessment constraints of current intelligence, it also has the ability to capture intelligence consumer attention in ways that more strategic analytical products struggle to emulate. It is always easier for intelligence organisations to make the case for their relevance and ability to inform policy with current intelligence than with longer-term forecasts or in-depth studies. The former ultimately come down to educated and sophisticated guesswork. And the latter may contribute to the institutional knowledge base and understanding but can appear remote and detached from policymaker priorities and urgencies so often dominated by news cycles and crisis response. The result is what Marrin refers to as a 'pendulum swing' in institutional priorities between prioritising current intelligence against more analytical products.[29] For example, a 1993 US intelligence community briefing to intelligence consumers listed more than three times as many intelligence community current intelligence products as either estimative or warning (21 current intelligence products from across the US intelligence community, compared with six each for estimative and warning intelligence).[30]

In military practice, current intelligence leans even more towards Kent's notion of 'reportorial' analysis and further from the standards and criteria of strategic assessment. The contribution of current intelligence is chiefly directed towards situational awareness, with timelines and deadlines largely driven by the prevailing tempo of operations. It is typically captured in an assortment of standardised products such as intelligence reports (INTREPs) that are issued 'whenever information or intelligence is urgent and contains any deductions that can be made in the time available'; 'concise, periodic' intelligence summaries, or INTSUM, that 'update the current intelligence picture' and 'highlight important developments'; and reinforced as needed by supplementary intelligence reports, or SUPINTREPs, that 'highlight important developments within the reporting cycle'.[31] Military doctrine acknowledges that current intelligence should rest on a well-informed and thorough underlying background understanding in the form of 'basic intelligence'.[32] But this is treated as a prescriptive guide rather than, après Marrin, a note of concern.

Sun Tzu, the legendary Chinese general of the sixth century BC, famously observed that 'all warfare is based on deception'.[33] Consequently, as Lord Butler has explained, 'intelligence may not differ in type or, often, reliability from other forms of information used by governments', but it 'operates in a field of particular difficulty' because '[by] definition the data it is trying to provide have been deliberately concealed'. As a consequence, 'the danger of deception must be considered' for all sources, technical or human.[34] The process by which intelligence reporting is examined to establish its reliability and possible adversary denial and deception is referred to as 'validation' in British intelligence practice, or 'evaluation' in NATO and US parlance.[35] Consequently, while *assessment* may not be essential to current intelligence, *validation* is.

It is important to appreciate the significance of validation in open-source intelligence (OSINT) in order to understand some of the issues in the timeliness and content that both Adam and Michaels identify. The availability of increasingly diverse, detailed real- and near-real-time sources of information conveyed by contemporary information and communication technologies has also entailed an equivalent expansion of the use of those technologies to misinform, malinform and disinform. Not only is the Russia–Ukraine war probably the most comprehensively and globally observed conflict, it is also equally arguably the conflict most comprehensively suffused with disinformation. The public has access to an unprecedented range and volume of detailed information matched in previous decades only by the resources of major national governments, with capabilities previously limited to national resources like highly capable reconnaissance satellites and globally deployed signals intelligence resources. At the same time, they are confronted with a miasma of systematic and technically highly sophisticated deception and manipulation. There are, of course, long-standing counter deception principles and techniques developed in the intelligence community which are as suitable to open-source exploitation as they are to national security capabilities.[36] But most citizens will have little access to or familiarity with these techniques – and even less time in their lives to acquire and apply them with the necessary rigour and consistency. There is, therefore, a premium on having some organisation or entity in a position to capture and validate the available open-source information, systematically collate it into a coherent appreciation, and winnow away the white noise and adversarial disinformation. This is what organisations like DI's analytic components exist in large part to do.

Viewed in terms of the conventions, requirements and interest that drive and shape military intelligence, one therefore has to view DI's daily Intelligence Update in different and analytically less ambitious terms than have so far prevailed. If we approach the Update as (mainly) a current intelligence product, we would not be asking what analytic depth and insight it offers so much as questions like:

1. How is it intended to update the existing picture and situational awareness?
2. On what kinds of change or lines of development is it reporting?
3. How effectively is it validating, collating and interpreting information to deliver (1) and (2)?
4. How effectively is it conveying that validated information?
5. Insofar as it does make inferences and analytical judgements, how accurate do those appreciations appear to have been?

This is not to say that current intelligence cannot offer analytic insight or touch on assessment, merely that this is not its principal *raison d'être*. In many respects, the interpretation and validation of information (raised in question 3) is essential to forming a clear judgement regarding the other criteria.

Rather than locating the DI Update within the narrative of declassification and disclosure, it is more useful to see it as part of an ongoing campaign to improve the exploitation of OSINT by DI and the wider intelligence community. Despite the enthusiasm for OSINT in recent decades, however, open-source has some real limitations. Almost by definition it is confined in its ability to penetrate a target's denial and deception measures and, at least in Britain, there is a strong case for arguing that the UK's national agencies were established specifically to provide what open sources could not.[37] The open domain is also the principal, large-scale and wide-coverage medium for propaganda, deception and disinformation. In the realm of the internet, it is also largely unregulated in terms of both volume and content. As a result, the search costs of OSINT are comparatively high (and increasing) because of the sheer volume of information that needs to be captured and sifted to identify relevant and reliable information, and to identify erroneous or deceptive materials. Because OSINT is not what intelligence doctrine calls a 'controlled source',[38] where the intelligence function can vouch for or has detailed insight into the origin and handling of the information, the validation task is especially demanding. To be sure, there is always the risk that a controlled source such as an agent has been doubled or that a satellite image is only of a decoy. But there will have been a vetting process in the recruitment of the human source and ongoing validation of their reporting, and imagery sensors are constantly evolving to find means to penetrate concealment or detect false signatures and decoys. But the web page, Telegram channel or other social media identity are often far more opaque in provenance while also embodying the same risks of hostile control, whether direct or indirect, conscious or unconscious.

The consequence of this is that OSINT validation *takes time*. Intelligence cannot simply take up and relay information in the open space the moment it appears and because it appears. The risks of hostile control, mischief, malice and sincere error must be taken into account. Sources need to have their *bona fides* evaluated, their provenance attributed, their content tested for corroboration, qualification or falsification. Open-source material will of course be discussed by the Update only days after it initially appears because of the validation process. Even as a purely OSINT product, without drawing on national security sources and capabilities, the Update would need processing time to validate and collate. It should be no surprise, therefore, that when the Update did finally detail the successful Ukrainian shooting down of a Russian Beriev A-50U ('Mainstay') air surveillance and early-warning aircraft and the damage to its attendant Ilyushin IL-22M ('Coot-B') airborne command post, it was almost three days after initial unconfirmed reports appeared in the public domain.[39] Battle damage reports are notoriously prone to error, premature confidence and exaggeration of success and significance. As a result, validation and confirmation are always a necessity, as is the time required to undertake them.

Adam and Michaels are almost certainly not wrong, however, when they speculate that the DI Update draws on classified sources in making its judgements. Using open-source information to convey knowledge gleaned from national security intelligence sources is a well-established practice often referred to as 'source masking'. Nearly two decades before the invasion of Ukraine, imagery analysts were using source masking to assist disaster relief efforts, for example locating survivors with national reconnaissance systems and then locating them in commercial imagery that could be provided to non-governmental organisations and relief agencies.[40] But insofar as the Update entails source masking and DI analysts look to classified sources to parse which open sources to trust and which not, that process of correlation and evaluation will still take time. There will, moreover, need to be a review and approval process before publication. And this will not happen in absolute real time. In fact, validating and reporting OSINT-based appreciations in the current disinformation environment in a day or three is impressively fast, even when there are classified sources to draw on to steer and confirm OSINT collation, validation, integration and exploitation, internal review and authorisation for release and publication.

In the purely technocratic terms of analytic tradecraft, perhaps the most problematic aspect of the Update, however, has been its use – and often abuse – of what the UK intelligence community refers to as 'conditional language'. Conditional language is terminology used to express levels of confidence in analytical judgements and the likelihood of those judgements being accurate. The issue of conditional language was first explicitly identified by Sherman Kent in terms of what he called 'words of estimative probability' (WEPs) in 1964.[41] Examining different sorts of uncertainty and consequent estimation in intelligence assessments, Kent observed that certain propositions in intelligence appreciations were factual statements while others were inferences, and that all inferences in intelligence carry with them a measure of uncertainty. He further asserted that the intelligence community 'should be able to choose a word or a phrase which quite accurately describes the degree of its certainty; and ideally, exactly this message should get through to the reader'.[42] The issue of conditional language and WEPs acquired a specific significance in the aftermath of the 2003 invasion of Iraq, when politicians in both the UK and USA criticised their respective intelligence communities for failing to make sufficiently clear their levels of uncertainty regarding appreciations of Iraqi non-conventional weapons capabilities. In fact, intelligence professionals had gone to some lengths to articulate their uncertainty, *but in terms that made sense to other intelligence professionals.* They employed conventions and terminology that were liable to misinterpretation and misrepresentation by politicians with different professional backgrounds and whose careers are defined by skills of persuasion rather than analysis.[43]

One of the key responses in Britain was an internal review of analytical methods used by DI, led by Stuart Jack. This resulted inter alia in the articulation of a body of formally prescribed language to express uncertainty, encapsulated in what was originally termed the 'Uncertainty Yardstick'.[44] Now into its second, revised version and rebranded the 'Probability Yardstick' (see *Figure 1*), the Yardstick prescribes very specific forms of language to express the probable accuracy of analytic judgements. Indeed, current UK analytic standards eschew the use of 'modal' ordinary language such as 'can', 'could', 'might' and 'may' and even 'possible' as the 'probabilistic equivalent of "weasel words"'.[45] Instead, analysts are to employ recommended phrases such as 'highly likely' and 'realistic possibility' to express specific measures of probability (75–85% and 25–50% respectively).

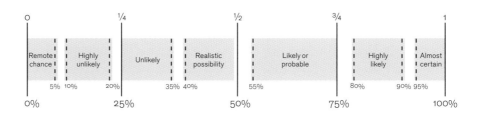

Figure 1

The most striking aspect of the Update's use of conditional language is how poorly it is incorporated into the drafting. Prescribed WEPs are often wedged into sentences with a complete absence of grammatical care and attention. We are informed, for example, that 'Since mid-September 2023, Russia has highly likely committed elements of its 25th

Combined Arms Army (25 CAA) to action for the very first time[46] or that 'Russia will highly likely need to reallocate SAMs [surface-to-air missiles] which are routinely protecting distant parts of Russia'.[47] In the first instance, such writing jars with one's sense of rhetorical nicety. 'Likely' is an adjective and not a mid-position adverb, and specifically one that ought to take a conjunction – it is likely that something is the case, or that that something is as likely as something else. 'It is highly likely that...' would be stylistically preferable, no less clear and make no real difference in time and effort during the writing. While the Yardstick might offer 'likely' and 'probably' as estimative equivalents, they are not directly sub-stitutable in grammatical terms. And 'probably' has the syntactical vir-tue of being a mid-position adverb. But the Update's authors scrupulously avoid its use. It is open to speculation why such an informal taboo seems to affect analytic drafting at DI, but a plausible reason is that confusion between 'possibly' and 'probably' was a recurrent theme in the post-Iraq deliberations that prompted the creation of the DI Yardstick.

Were it simply a problem of awkward prose it would hardly warrant significant concern, but in some cases the perfunctory use of condi-tional language obscures the intended analytical message. On 17 January 2023, discussing Russian use of long-range missiles against civilian infrastructure during the winter, the Update asserted that 'An AS-4 KITCHEN large anti-ship missile, launched from a TU23M3 BACKFIRE medium bomber, highly likely struck a block of flats in Dnipro City which resulted in the death of at least 40 people.'[48] This leaves the reader puzzling as to whether it was highly likely (85%) that the block of flats was struck, and so leaving some possibility, however 'highly unlikely' (10–15%), that the building had not been hit at all. Or whether it was highly likely that it was this strike that caused the tragic loss of life rather than some other cause. Or if it was highly likely that it was an AS-4 that hit as opposed to some other type of missile. A reader might even ask why the Update's authors were so certain the missile in question was launched from a BACKFIRE bomber rather than some other class of aircraft. A clearer form of writing would have been 'It is highly likely that the missile which struck a block of flats in the city of Dnipro, resulting in the deaths of 40 people, was an AS-4 KITCHEN large anti-ship missile launched from a TU23M3 BACKFIRE medium bomber.' Four more words seem a small enough increased word length to exchange for significantly clearer writing.

In fairness, there are instances of tidier language in the Update. On 13 October 2023, for example, it noted a hiatus in Russian long-range aviation (LRA) airstrikes between 9 March and 28 April, saying it was 'likely that the LRA had almost depleted its stocks' of AS-23 KODIAK air-to-surface missiles.[49] However, there have also been times where conditional language has been used as a sort of default phrasing or filler. When the Update reported on 1 November 2023 that 'Russia's Lancet small one-way-attack uncrewed aerial systems (OWA UAVs) have highly likely been one of the most effective new capabilities Russia has fielded…over the last 12 months',[50] one has to ask where the analytic uncertainty lies in this judgement. One might as easily say the Lancet is 'amongst the most effective' without losing accuracy or rigour.

The point in all this is not simply to play the role of authoritarian grammarian, but to make two significant, linked points about what the Update may be telling us about more pervasive issues in the conduct of intelligence analysis within DI. The most important of these is that what we see in the use of conditional language in the Update is not the scrupulous use and articulation of carefully evaluated levels of uncertainty. In 1964, Kent warned analysts that they should try to use WEPs 'sparingly and in places where they are least likely to obscure the thrust of our key estimative passages'.[51] Instead, in the Update, prescribed expressions are frequently parachuted into sentences in a perfunctory fashion. What we see in the Update is not WEPs as instruments of analytic rigour but exercises in formal compliance and the box-ticking of professional standards. The second point follows from the argument above that the Update is written in terms of, and employs, the standards and conventions of military intelligence, drafting in general and current intelligence reporting practice in particular. From this it follows that it is – pardon the phrase – *highly likely* that the analytic drafting style and practice we see in the Update is indicative of the style and practice in common use throughout DI analytic production. In other words, there is a *high probability* that the use of conditional language detached from analytic process and employed as a perfunctory formal compliance is a wider, even pervasive practice amongst DI analysts. This would defeat the purpose for which prescribed conditional language and the DI Yardstick were intended. And if this is so, it would be a source of serious concern regarding the possible quality of classified DI analytic processes and products.

In due course, many other questions will need to be asked of the DI Daily Update, particularly around the accuracy of its analytical judgements – its 'batting average', as American commentators have put it.[52] There will inevitably have been miscalls as well as accurate appreciations over the course of the conflict, as there are in intelligence in any crisis. And these will need to be examined in closer detail once the conflict has reached a conclusion and we are in a better position to piece together what exactly was happening, and once the thickest residual fog of war has dispersed. In the meantime, the daily update will be of best use to its intended audience if approached on its own terms rather than with expectations drawn from entirely different levels and forms of analytic product. Even accepted on those terms, however, it is possible to detect indications of systemic issues of professional practice affecting it. To be sure, the Update is, as many have noted, a somewhat unprecedented experiment, and undoubtedly its drafters are learning as they go. But clear analytic drafting and the use of post-Iraq, post-Butler refinements in analytic tradecraft are neither new nor experimental. Both the public and governmental consumers of DI products should be able to expect analytic standards to be above formal compliance – and certainly beyond what the observance of what organisational sociologists John W Meyer and Brian Rowan have referred to as bureaucratic 'myth and ceremony'.[53]

1. Douglas J MacEachin. The tradecraft of analysis. In Roy Godson, Ernest R May and Gary Schmitt (eds.), *US Intelligence at the Crossroads: Agendas for Reform*. Washington DC: Brassey's, 1995, pp. 63–74.

2. Karla Adam. How U.K. intelligence came to tweet the lowdown on the war in Ukraine. *Washington Post*, 22 April 2022, https://www.washingtonpost.com/world/2022/04/22/how-uk-intelligence-came-tweet-lowdown-war-ukraine/.

3. 'Declassified' refers to material that at some point was classified but has had its caveat rescinded, while 'unclassified' refers to something originally issued without any protective security marking.

4. Jeffrey Michaels. Ukraine: the daily intelligence event. *RUSI Commentary*, 18 May 2022, https://rusi.org/explore-our-research/publications/commentary/ukraine-daily-intelligence-event.

5. Ibid.

6. See eg John Prados (ed.), *The White House Tapes: Eavesdropping on the President*. New York: New Press, 2003, pp. 92–7. Contra Michaels' assertion about the US intelligence community assessing a corrupt South Vietnamese regime, see eg Director of Central Intelligence (DCI) and United States Intelligence Board (USIB), National Intelligence Estimate, number 53–63: prospects in South Vietnam, 17 April 1963 (declassified January 2005), https://www.cia.gov/readingroom/docs/DOC_0001166413.pdf..

7. On net assessment, see Philip H J Davies, *Intelligence and Government in Britain and the United States, Volume 1: Evolution of the US Intelligence Community*. Santa Barbara, CA: Praeger Security International, 2012, pp. 180–1, 256. On the Secretary of State's Office of Net Assessment and Challenge (SONAC) see eg Ministry of Defence, Announcement of new Director appointed to the Secretary of State's Office of Net Assessment and Challenge (press release), 6 May 2022, https://www.gov.uk/government/news/announcement-of-new-director-appointed-to-the-secretary-of-states-office-for-net-assessment-and-challenge-sonac; Gabriel Elefteriu, The MoD's newly independent 'net assessment' capability can make a huge difference. *Policy Exchange*, 18 January 2022, https://policyexchange.org.uk/blogs/the-mods-newly-independent-net-assessment-capability-can-make-a-huge-difference/.

8. On the command staff division of labour see eg Michael I Handel, Intelligence and military operations, in Michael I Handel (ed.), *Intelligence and Military Operations*. London: Frank Cass, 1990, pp. 21–32.

9. Senate Select Committee to Study Governmental Operations with Respect to Intelligence Activities. *Final Report of the Senate Select Committee to Study Governmental Operations with Respect to Intelligence Activities United States Senate Together with Additional, Supplemental, and Separate Views*, 7 vols, Report No 94-753, 94th Congress. Washington, DC: United States Government Printing Office, 1976. https://www.intelligence.senate.gov/sites/default/files/94755_II.pdf.

10. See, variously, Lord Franks, *Falkland Islands Review: Report of a Committee of Privy Counsellors*. London: HMSO, 1983; Percy Cradock, *Know Your Enemy: How the Joint*

Intelligence Committee Saw the World. London: John Murray (Publishers) Ltd, 2002; Lord Butler, *Review of Intelligence on Weapons of Mass Destruction.* London: The Stationery Office, 2004; Michael S Goodman, *The Official History of the Joint Intelligence Committee, Volume 1: From the Approach of the Second World War to the Suez Crisis.* London: Routledge, 2016; and the report and proceedings of Sir John Chilcot's Iraq Inquiry at https://webarchive.nationalarchives.gov.uk/ukgwa/20171123123237/http://www.iraqinquiry.org.uk//.

11. Davies, *Intelligence and Government, Volume 1*, p. 64.

12. Quoted in Philip H J Davies, Organizational politics and the development of Britain's intelligence producer/consumer interface, *Intelligence and National Security*, vol 10, no 4, October 1995, p. 113.

13. For a concise description of estimative intelligence, see eg Office of the Director of Central Intelligence (ODCI), *A Consumer's Guide to Intelligence* OPAI 93-00092. Washington DC: ODCI, 1993. More detailed discussions of estimative intelligence can be found in eg Harold P Ford, *Estimative Intelligence: the Purposes and Problems of National Intelligence Estimating.* Lanham, MD: University Press of America, 1993; or Sherman Kent, Estimates and influence, *Studies in Intelligence*, vol 12, no 3, 1968, pp. 11–21.

14. Butler, *Review of Intelligence*, p. 10.

15. Professional Head of Intelligence Assessment, *Professional Development Framework for All-Source Intelligence Assessment.* London: Cabinet Office, 2019, p. 6.

16. Butler, *Review of Intelligence*, pp. 10–11.

17. Development, Concepts and Doctrine Centre (DCDC). *Joint Doctrine Publication 2-00: Intelligence, Counterintelligence and Security Support to Joint Operations*, 4th edn. Shrivenham, UK: DCDC, 2023, p. 30.

18. ODCI, *Consumer's Guide to Intelligence*, p. 4.

19. Practical examples of this may be found in the JIC Watch Manuals that have been released to the National Archive, ie JIC Watch Manual, JIC(62)29 (Final), 20 April 1957; and JIC Watch Manual, JIC(62)29 (Final), both in CAB 158/45, and JIC Watch Manual, INT 42(74)1 (working draft), 31 January 1974, CAB 190/71.

20. See eg Sherman Kent, *A crucial estimate relived, Studies in Intelligence*, vol 36, no 5, 1964, pp. 111–19.

21. Lawrence Freedman. *The Official History of the Falklands Campaign: Revised and Updated Edition, Volume 1: The Origins of the Falklands War.* London: Routledge, 2005, esp pp. 162, 204, 207; John Ferris. *Behind the Enigma: the Authorised History of GCHQ, Britain's Cyber-Intelligence Agency.* London: Bloomsbury, 2020, pp. 615–24.

22. Sherman Kent. *Strategic Intelligence for US World Policy*, 2nd edn. Princeton, NJ: Princeton University Press, 1965 [1949], p. 29.

23. Ibid, p. 30.

24. Ibid, p. 38.

25. For a closer examination of the central but underacknowledged significance of tasking and priorities, see Neveen S Abdalla and Philip H J Davies, Intelligence

and the mandate: a third form of strategic failure. *International Journal of Intelligence, Security and Public Affairs*, vol 23, no 2, 2021, pp. 105–24.

26. Stephen Marrin. *Improving Intelligence Analysis: Bridging the Gap Between Scholarship and Practice*. London: Routledge, 2011, p. 17.

27. Ibid, p. 64.

28. Ibid, p. 85.

29. Ibid, pp. 62–7.

30. ODCI, *Consumer's Guide to Intelligence*, pp. 21–6. The *Guide* describes 21 current intelligence products, occupying 4 out of 6 pages, from across the community, compared with 6 each for estimative and warning intelligence.

31. DCDC, *Joint Doctrine Publication 2-00*, p. 71.

32. Ibid, p. 30.

33. Sun Tzu, trans Samuel B Griffith. *The Art of War*. London: Oxford University Press, 1971 [1963], p. 66.

34. Butler, *Review of Intelligence*, p. 9.

35. Ibid, pp. 9–10; DCDC; *Joint Doctrine Publication 2-00*, pp. 58–9.

36. See eg James B Bruce and Michael Bennett, Foreign denial and deception: analytical imperatives, in James B Bruce and Roger Z George (eds), *Analyzing Intelligence: Origins, Obstacles, and Innovations*. Washington DC: Georgetown University Press, 2008, pp. 122–37; and Richards J Heuer Jr and Randolph H Pherson, *Structured Analytics for Intelligence Analysis*. Washington DC: CQ Press, 2011, pp. 173–5.

37. Davies, *Intelligence and Government*, Volume 1, pp. 44–69.

38. DCDC, *Joint Doctrine Publication 2-00*, p. 47.

39. DI. Update on Ukraine 17 January: intelligence update, https://twitter.com/DefenceHQ/status/1747544627257745426; Oliver Slow, Ukraine says it shot down a Russian A50 spy plane, BBC News, 15 January 2024, https://www.bbc.co.uk/news/world-europe-67978739. Significantly, a second A-50U was downed a month later and the Update again confirmed this two days afterwards.

40. See eg, Committee on the future US workforce for geospatial intelligence, *Future US Workforce for Geospatial Reference*. Washington DC: National Academies Press, 2013, p. 14.

41. Sherman Kent. Words of estimative probability. *Studies in Intelligence*, vol 8, no 4, 1964, pp. 49–65.

42. Ibid, p. 64.

43. Davies, *Intelligence and Government*, Volume 1, pp. 388–95; *Intelligence and Government,* Volume 2, pp. 76–279.

44. For the first edition see eg DCDC, *Understanding and Intelligence Support to Joint Operations*, 3rd edn. Shrivenham, UK: DCDC, 2011, pp. 2–23, revised in the 4th edn, op cit, p. 65. See also Professional Head of Defence Intelligence Analysis (PHDIA), *Quick Wins for Busy Analysts*. London: Defence Intelligence, 2016, pp. 55, 58–9.

45. PHDIA, *Quick Wins*, p. 58.

46. DI. Update on Ukraine 27 September 2023: intelligence update, https:twitter.com/DefenceHQ/status/1706903544190689630.
47. DI. Update on Ukraine 09 November 2023: intelligence update, https:twitter.com/DefenceHQ/status/1722540708681195856.
48. DI. Update on Ukraine 10 January 2023: intelligence update, https:twitter.com/DefenceHQ/status/1615234018164760576.
49. DI. Update on Ukraine 13 October 2023: intelligence update, https:twitter.com/DefenceHQ/status/1712702484446158861.
50. DI. Update on Ukraine 01 November 2023: intelligence update, https:twitter.com/DefenceHQ/status/1719621502121775113.
51. Sherman Kent. Words of estimative probability. CIA, 1964, p. 64 *infra*.
52. See, inter alia, Stephen Marrin, Evaluating the quality of intelligence analysis: by what (mis)measure? *Intelligence and National Security*, vol 27, no 6, 2012, pp. 1–17; and Jim Marchio, How good is your 'batting average'? Early IC efforts to assess the accuracy of estimates. Studies in Intelligence, vol 60, no 4, 2016, pp. 3–13.
53. John W Meyer and Brian Rowan. Institutionalized organizations: formal structure as myth and ceremony. *American Journal of Sociology*, vol 83, no 2, 1977, pp. 340–63.

Engineering students in a classroom at the Patrice Lumumba Friendship University in Moscow, 1961.

A FAUSTIAN BARGAIN: MOSCOW'S COVERT ALLIANCES IN AFRICA, FROM THE COLD WAR TO THE PRESENT

Daniela Richterova

'Russia is returning to Africa. We were present in many countries during the time of the Soviet Union, and Russia is coming back to the same position. We still have connections and we are trying to re-establish them.'

VALERY ZAKHAROV, former GRU (Russian military intelligence) officer and Chechnya veteran installed as the Central African Republic's national security adviser, 2019.[1]

Since 2017, Russian-speaking soldiers and security advisers have become a permanent fixture in a number of African states, often war-stricken ones. These enigmatic figures were no official envoys of the Russian Federation attached to Moscow's embassies. They were seemingly independent actors initially lacking a designated uniform or insignia. Soon, however, an ominous-looking symbol made up of a human skull set against a black-and-red backdrop symbolising victory over death started appearing on posters, flags and the flexed biceps of these camera-shy Russian-speaking warriors. The so-called Wagner Network was slowly emerging from the shadows and leaving its finger-prints on an increasing number of operations across the continent.

By 2023 a lot had changed. The increasingly confident founders of the Kremlin's private army, Yevgeny Prigozhin and Dmitry Utkin, were dead. They died mysterious deaths not long after their failed June 2023 mutiny attempt and march on Moscow. Soon afterwards, the group was cleansed of its toxic label and renamed the Africa Corps. At the same time, Moscow tightened the reins over its Frankenstein creation which was originally designed to pursue Russian covert foreign policy and economic gain in a secret and deniable way, bringing it under closer control of the Ministry of Defence.[2]

Throughout this crisis, however, Moscow's mercenaries continued to operate and expand the country's presence in Africa. While our knowledge of the nature of Africa Corps operations on the continent remains limited, Moscow's mercenaries – including Valery Zakharov – have maintained that there is nothing new to see here; that since 2017, Wagner has merely been trying to revive old Cold War connections. This paper challenges this narrative. By comparing Moscow's Cold War military, security and intelligence (MSI) engagement in Africa with that of Moscow's engagement on the continent via the Wagner Network and now Africa Corps, it argues that, under Putin, the Kremlin has crossed Cold War red lines in important ways, namely by aiming to 'state-capture' their allies, engaging in direct combat and perpetrating human rights abuses.

This piece draws on research into Soviet Bloc engagement in the Global South largely based on unique documents from Central and Eastern European archives. These works show the nature of Moscow and its allies' MSI engagement in and with Africa during the Cold War. Thanks to this rich material, which details discussions between key stakeholders, as well as the nature of and challenges to providing assistance, we are now able to better understand where Moscow and its allies drew red lines in terms of MSI engagement – boundaries beyond which they were not willing to go.[3] When analysing Moscow's Putin-era MSI support for Africa, this piece relies on Western government reports into Wagner/ Africa Corps operations, journalistic investigations and the testimonies of Wagner defectors.

While the Soviet Union's interest in the Global South dates back to the Stalin era, Moscow first created significant ties with the continent during the Khrushchev years.[4] In the mid-1950s, amid decolonisation, Khrushchev called for a political and cultural offensive towards non-allied countries, many of which were in Africa. At the centre of this new strategy was a mixture of overt and covert support, aimed at improving the economic situation of African partners and modernising their military and security establishments. This combined strategy became key to Moscow's fight against colonialism and imperialism.

In the early 1960s, to enable this new foreign policy towards the Global South, the Soviet Union reformed its government infrastructure. Academic institutes were established in an effort to develop expertise in these regions. The Communist Party set up two new departments focusing on international affairs and foreign Communist parties. Part of this campaign was the creation of the prestigious Moscow-based Patrice Lumumba University, designed to host like-minded students from across the Global South.[5] Moreover, the country's intelligence community – both the KGB civilian security and intelligence organisation and the GRU, the Soviet Union's military intelligence outfit – were reorganised to help facilitate this new policy.[6] Similar reforms took place across the Soviet Bloc. Moscow's overt as well as covert assistance to Africa and other Global South countries was complemented by that of its closest and most capable allies, who ran their own programmes in support of the same goals: Czechoslovakia was Moscow's most experienced arms producer and exporter , and in the 1960s developed extensive training facilities; the German Democratic Republic was not a major arms exporter but provided substantial MSI training and strategic advice; and Poland also provided arms and training to these new allies.[7]

Moscow and its satellites had good reasons to pursue partnerships with non-aligned African nations. First, they wanted to have presence across the globe and especially at critical junctures such as ports in the Indian Ocean. Second, by having presence on the ground, they hoped to project their influence onto governments and local Communist parties. Third, by creating these strongholds, Moscow sought to deter their ideological enemies in the West from winning the allegiance of non-allied states. China, who also sought to project its influence onto African governments at the time, was to be deterred from creating a foothold in key regions.[8] Fourth, economic reasons also drove the Soviet Bloc's policy, namely its constant need for foreign currency, which could have been acquired by doing business with countries outside the Bloc. The weight of each of these factors changed over time – most notably in the latter part of the Cold War, when influence and geopolitics gave way to the need for hard currency and profit.[9]

During the Cold War, the Soviet Bloc established relations with over three dozen African countries.[10] While some were brief affairs, others lasted for decades and brought significant benefits to both sides. They ranged across the continent from Morocco, Algeria, Egypt and Libya, through Ghana, Guinea, Mali, Congo and Ethiopia, to Nigeria, Somalia and Angola. To cast its web widely, ideological proximity to Marxism–Leninism was welcome, but it was not a condition for aid. While some of

The construction of the Aswan
Dam on the Nile, Egypt, 1968.

Moscow's African partners struck alliances in times of peace, others did so in times of heightened security threats (Egypt) or during an ongoing civil war (Nigeria).[11] In addition to states, Moscow also became a loud advocate of myriad African national liberation movements. At the United Nations and other international fora, it advocated for these movements and their just fight against oppressive colonisers.[12]

Moscow and its allies provided crucial overt support to their partners on the African continent. They extended their political and diplomatic backing to African leaders who ascended to power during the era of decolonisation and were looking to consolidate their often fragile grip on power. Economic assistance and investment were at the heart of this overt assistance. Moscow and its allies typically encouraged nationalisation of foreign assets, support for local industries, strengthening the state sector in respective countries, and (often radical) sector-wide reforms. In addition to this, the Soviet Union extended generous financial aid, donating $100 million to Algeria, $81m to Ghana and $80m to Guinea.[13]

To (re)build often poor infrastructure and modernise their countries, large-scale investment deals were forged which saw the Soviets and their allies build hundreds of enterprises, factories and plants across the continent, including the Aswan Dam, crucial for Egypt's agriculture and energy supply; the Capanda Dam, a hydroelectric dam which provides most of Angola with electricity; as well as plants in Congo and Nigeria. African regimes and groups also accepted generous financial aid packages from the Soviet Bloc, some in the form of financial credit, others in the form of direct donations. Finally, these alliances also carried a cultural component. To educate and influence new African elites, between 1949 and 1991, approximately 60,000 Africans studied in the USSR, engaging in student exchanges, training and language courses.[14]

Covert assistance was a crucial component of these new alliances. In fact, Soviet Bloc MSI support to Africa was in many instances the 'gateway drug' to establishing broader collaboration with African leaders. National security was on top of many states' agendas, as it became crucial to the survival of newly independent and revolutionary states. The old colonial defence and security sectors they inherited were, however, in many cases decimated and unfit to fulfil these needs. Moreover, because during the colonial era these sensitive portfolios had typically been run by Europeans, the new postcolonial elites lacked proper experience and training. To secure their power, break with their colonial past and achieve adequate capability, African states in many cases had to build their MSI establishments from scratch. They were in dire need of well-equipped militaries and security establishments, up-to-standard trained troops and security personnel, and the necessary weapons and MSI technology to overcome threats to sovereignty.

The Soviet Bloc's covert assistance to African partners was a delicate venture, exclusively handled by state and Communist Party institutions: representatives of the military and security services negotiated MSI contracts; defence and interior ministries provided training and at times also strategic advice in theatre to those states and non-state actors engaged in conflicts. State-owned arms companies played a crucial role, supplying weapons to allies on the continent on a mostly commercial basis.[15] All had to be approved by the powerful International Department of the Communist Party, in charge of crafting the country's foreign policy.[16]

The Soviet Bloc's first large arms deal with the Global South was struck with Gamal Abdel Nasser's Egypt. After years of failed attempts to purchase weapons from the West and increasing clashes with Israel, in September 1955 Cairo struck a landmark deal with Czechoslovakia, Moscow's close ally. An experienced global arms provider, Prague sold an assortment of military aircraft, tanks, boats, armoured vehicles, cannons and other smaller weapons to the North African country. Worth $45.7m, Czechoslovakia received 80% of the sum in goods, mostly cotton, and the rest in hard currency, underwritten by a Soviet loan to Cairo. During the next two years further deals with Prague and Moscow followed, and by 1957 the two Soviet Bloc states were responsible for 85% of Egypt's military imports.[17]

Where Soviet Bloc jets, tanks and guns went, training followed. This took place both in Africa and in the Soviet Bloc, where specialised facilities to accommodate this demand were built. Under Brezhnev, Moscow established a large training facility called Perevalnoe, opened in Crimea in 1965 and dedicated mostly to training African revolutionaries, and also trained cadets at other locations near Moscow as well as on the Black Sea coast in Georgia.[18] East Germany trained military and security cadets from Mozambique and Ethiopia, and also those from the ANC (African National Congress).[19] Soviet Bloc states also assisted in designing curricula and building training facilities overseas. For instance, apart from training African soldiers and spies at home as well as in their home countries, Prague helped design Egypt's military education programmes at the Military Engineering faculty of the University of Alexandria.[20] Thousands of special advisers were also dispatched to select Global South governments and nationalist movements to advise on military strategy and organisation. Their role became particularly important during times of crisis; whether during the 1969–70 war of attrition between Egypt and Israel in which thousands of Soviet technicians operated sophisticated radar and surface-to-air missiles, or during national liberation struggles, when Soviet Bloc advisers attempted to influence the strategy and tactics of national liberation movements, achieving mixed results.[21]

While the Soviet Bloc's covert assistance to African actors during the Cold War was substantial, Moscow and its allies drew red lines beyond which they were not willing to go. A thick red line was drawn at direct engagement in conflict. While Moscow and its partners were happy to provide arms, training and advice, they steered away from participating in armed conflicts waged by their African allies.[22] They were not willing to fight someone else's wars.

Thirty years after the end of the Cold War, Moscow continues to use a mixture of overt and covert engagement to sustain alliances and project influence in Africa. These days, however, it *is* willing to fight someone else's wars. By deploying a variety of crypto-state proxies, seemingly private companies linked to key ministries, Putin has crossed the thick red line drawn by his predecessors during the Cold War.

Since the fall of the Berlin Wall, Russia's relationship with Africa has gone through a number of phases: while in the early 1990s it largely came to a standstill, by the time Vladimir Putin became president in 2000, Moscow was gradually rekindling its ties with the strategically important continent.[23] It was, however, not until the mid-2000s, when the rift between Russia and the West was re-emerging as a consequence of the colour revolutions in Georgia and Ukraine as well as the war in Iraq, that Russia's policy towards Africa and the rest of the Global South became more activist. With a 'politically blind' and 'no strings attached' approach, Russia soon started forging Cold War-style alliances with pro- as well as anti-Western states including Libya, Sudan and Zimbabwe. By the time Putin took the presidential mantle from Dmitry Medvedev and started his third term in office in 2012, the world had changed yet again. Following the Arab Spring and a definitive collapse of US–Russia dialogue, Putin used anti-Westernism as the key ingredient for striking new alliances and recalibrating old ones.[24]

By the late 2010s, following Moscow's 2014 annexation of Crimea and 2018 military intervention in Syria on behalf of the Assad government, Russian foreign policy turned yet further away from the West and towards the Global South. Africa thus became a key region of confrontation between Russia and the West. Where the US, France and other Western allies suspended operations or imposed sanctions, Russia moved in. The year 2015 was a key one for the expansion of Moscow's security presence on the continent. Over the ensuing two years, Russia signed significant economic and MSI agreements with Zimbabwe, Ghana, Rwanda, Gambia, Mozambique, Chad, Niger and Nigeria.[25] At the same time, Russia turned to another trick in its Cold War-era playbook – projecting soft power through multimillion-dollar loan and aid packages to some of the most deprived countries on the continent, including the Central African Republic (CAR) and South Sudan.[26] In 2019, Putin put Russia's extensive ties with African states on full display at the Russia–Africa Summit, which had alone allegedly generated business deals amounting to $12.5 billion.[27]

The resurgence of Russian assistance to Africa over the past decade has been motivated by numerous factors. From the Russian perspective, this engagement served as a means to assert and demonstrate the nation's enduring status as a global power and to confront its key adversaries – namely NATO, the US and France – in a distant theatre.[28] Additionally, it presented an opportunity to advance President Putin's vision of a post-liberal international world order, positioning Russia as a key player in shaping global dynamics. The pursuit of economic gains, particularly considering Western sanctions imposed in 2014 after Moscow's annexation of Crimea, constituted another driving factor, as Russia sought avenues to mitigate the impact of those sanctions. Moscow's desire to influence global opinion during its war in Ukraine was arguably also a factor.

Conversely, African nations had their own unique mix of reasons that led them to seek Russian support. The prospect of a sponsor without strings attached appealed to African countries, providing them with a source of assistance devoid of conditions. Moreover, this engagement offered critical support for regimes or leaders facing internal crises, bolstering their stability and resilience. In the broader geopolitical context, aligning with Russia allowed African nations to diversify their alliances and potentially gain leverage in global affairs, particularly during periods of heightened global tensions or conflict.

While Russia was gradually ticking off more and more boxes in its Cold War-era playbook, it added new features to its engagement in Africa. Crucially, it deployed seemingly private military companies to foster ties with some of its most notorious customers in a strategic way. These were not merely deployed to mimic existing state-to-state ties, but were set to considerably broaden the extent and level of risk associated with Moscow's operations. By 2017, to maximise its profit from alliances with the most authoritarian and troubled regimes on the continent, Russia deviated from its Cold War doctrine.

The first notable difference in Putin-era engagement with Africa has been the type of actors Moscow deployed to strengthen its alliance. During the Cold War, these complex relations were explicitly handled by state and Communist Party representatives, but in 2017 Russia began to pursue a two-tier strategy. On the one hand, it continued to foster direct state-to-state relations with many African countries, directly managed by Russian ministries and state arms companies. On the other, since the late 2010s, it had increasingly been using non-state private military companies with links to the Russian Ministry of Defence to pursue its most controversial alliances on the continent and to provide controversial services. Arguably, this strategic shift from exclusive state-to-state to crypto-state organisations handling these alliances was introduced to afford Russia plausible deniability, facilitate swift deployment and allow the flexibility to undertake higher-risk operations.[29]

Russia began using its mercenaries to reassert its position across the continent in Putin's third presidential term. Moscow's first proxy-led sustained military presence in Africa commenced in 2017, in the CAR and Sudan. Subsequently, in 2018, crypto-state companies were used to strengthen Russian ties with Guinea and Libya, and there are indications of ongoing long-term missions in Mozambique, Mali and Burkina Faso.[30] The Russian mercenaries who arrived in Africa featured both experienced managers, often comprising former Russian military personnel overseeing training programmes, and rank-and-file operatives, including former soldiers and individuals with varying levels of expertise. In a nod to the Soviet era, when Soviet Bloc states collaborated in their overtures towards Africa, Putin's proxy teams were composed of personnel from countries such as Ukraine, Belarus, Serbia and other post-Soviet states.[31]

While ostensibly presenting themselves as independent entities, Russian proxies maintained a substantial reliance on the infrastructure of the Russian state. Testimonies from former Wagner fighters shed light on the extensive military support provided by the Russian government to the Wagner Network since its inception. They detail how all essential combat resources, including uniforms, equipment, weapons and ammunition, were sourced directly from Ministry of Defence stocks. Even the standard-issue weapon for Wagner fighters, a 5.45 mm machine gun, depended on the continuous supply of ammunition facilitated by the Russian state. The Ministry also provided essential logistics support, facilitating the transport of Wagner operatives and lightweight cargo to conflict zones in Africa. These revelations underscore the intricate linkages between seemingly independent proxy networks and the state apparatus, emphasising the extensive state backing that underpinned their operational capabilities.[32]

This shift to mercenary territory has also had an impact on the way Wagner and later the Africa Corps have used overt and covert means to pursue influence. While during the latter part of the 20th century the Kremlin sold weapons, training and advice to African partners, typically at commercial prices, it combined its MSI assistance with long-term development programmes characterised by educational and cultural support, financial aid and extensive investment in critical infrastructure. The goal here was not to take the resources away from the newly established African regimes, but to strengthen the standing of the leaders they aligned with, assist them in developing key sectors and the social capital of their populations and, in return, gain their political allegiance, loyalty and cash. The Soviet Union was assisting in building African empires, which would in turn become their allies.

In a second notable Putin-era shift, this model has been turned upside down. In pursuit of the same goals – political allegiance, loyalty and cash – mercenaries have effectively been building their own empires within partner African states. Some have characterised this approach as 'state capture', signifying a multifaceted strategy that manipulates state institutions and decision-making processes to serve its own interests. This approach extends beyond conventional military and economic engagements, aiming to influence the balance of power and governance structures in African nations. The Wagner-turned-Africa Corps' state capture strategy is predominantly centred around providing military, security and intelligence assistance to failing or fragile regimes in exchange for Faustian bargains. These endow the Kremlin's proxy companies with ownership of local companies, exclusive mining rights to key natural resource reserves, and influence through media manipulation.

Russia's state capture strategy encompasses economic endeavours, including investments in breweries and vodka distilleries. By securing stakes in these sectors, Russia can exert economic influence and potentially leverage these assets for political gains, creating dependencies and fostering a broader sphere of control. The state capture concept is particularly prominent in discussions surrounding countries like the CAR, where, for years, primarily through the activities of the Wagner Network, Moscow engaged in a complex set of hybrid activities.[33] The gateway to Russia's state capture of the CAR was MSI training of the country's armed forces. In 2017, Moscow's mercenaries arrived in the republic to train the country's armed forces, who were facing an insurgency by rebels challenging the rule of the sitting president. Soon, they were engaged in direct combat and personal protection of the country's top leadership. In return, Moscow's mercenaries gained exclusive extraction rights to gold, diamonds and rare timber allegedly worth hundreds of millions of dollars. Wagner representatives also set up a thriving local brewery, producing the Africa Ti L'Or beer, and a local radio station designed to promote the Russian mercenary mission.[34]

In addition to this exploitation, there is growing evidence that Russia's strategy extends to smuggling operations aimed at circumventing international sanctions and supporting its military effort in Ukraine. In Sudan, for instance, approximately 90% of the extracted gold, worth around $13.4bn, is allegedly being smuggled out of the country, with evidence suggesting that Moscow began extracting gold in the region as early as 2014, following the annexation of Crimea.[35] This economic exploitation aligns with Wagner's original tactical approach, aimed at targeting countries with valuable natural resources in order to advance Moscow's objectives.

The third key shift in the Kremlin's strategy has been in how far it is willing to go in providing MSI assistance to its African allies. Prior to 1989, Moscow's core covert business in Africa involved the provision of arms, training and advice to often weak governments and non-state

Vladimir Putin with African leaders,
St Petersburg, Russia, July 2023.

actors leading insurgencies against colonial or otherwise oppressive governments. Russia continues to provide this to its African allies. Under Putin, African partner states have received arms largely via the state-to-state route. In fact, in recent years, Russia has emerged as Africa's largest arms supplier, accounting for a substantial percentage of major arms imports. Between 2017 and 2021, Russia contributed 44% of Africa's imports of major arms, signifying a significant role in the region's military capabilities.[36] Russia's long-standing MSI training programmes also continue to form the heart of their alliances. These are often carried out by Moscow's proxy companies. As part of these training initiatives, around 250 Russian mercenaries were involved in training army recruits in the CAR, while in Sudan, military, intelligence, special forces and the paramilitary group known as the Rapid Support Forces also received training.[37] Additionally, in Libya, military training was provided to Haftar forces.[38]

While there is continuity in arms provision and training, Moscow's Putin-era covert assistance has crossed that metaphorical Cold War-era red line. Via Wagner and now the Africa Corps, the Kremlin is providing protection services for its allies on the continent. These include surveillance and physical protection. In Sudan, the Kremlin's proxies provided surveillance and protection for key sites and officials; in Libya, they secured oil sites, showcasing Russia's new role in safeguarding critical infrastructure. The construction of military infrastructure is another aspect of Russia's involvement, as evidenced in Libya, where Russia has been involved in building command-and-control systems in military bases and logistics bridges connecting the region to the Sahel, Sub-Saharan Africa and potentially Ukraine. Furthermore, these crypto-state companies have run social media for pro-Rapid Support Forces in Sudan and provided political advisory services coupled with social media influence operations in Libya.[39] Additionally, discreditation campaigns targeting journalists, as observed in the case of CNN preparing a report on Russia's activities in the CAR, highlight a tactic employed to manipulate public perception and control the narrative.[40]

The most notable shift from its Cold War doctrine, however, pertains to direct combat. While the Soviet Union drew a clear red line at direct engagement in local conflicts in the African continent, Putin-era mercenaries have marched straight through it and are now fighting African wars. They deploy their men into various types of combat and crisis situations. One avenue is direct military involvement, exemplified by its specialised military operations in Libya since 2018. In this scenario, Moscow's proxies aligned themselves with the LNA (Libyan National Army), aiding General Khalifa Haftar's forces in their campaign against Islamist militants in eastern Libya. In April 2019, the group also extended its support to Haftar's failed offensive on Tripoli, challenging the UN-backed government.[41] Furthermore, Moscow's mercenaries have demonstrated a propensity for active involvement in supporting coups, as witnessed in Sudan in 2021, where mercenaries played a role in the overthrow of the civilian government.[42] Additionally, Russian proxies have been engaged in operations against local insurgents, exemplified in the CAR, where it has contributed to counterinsurgency efforts. This multifaceted engagement reflects the group's adaptability in crisis contexts, employing military interventions and support for coups to further Russia's strategic and economic objectives. Crucially, it shows that it is willing to take on much higher risk to secure these alliances and substantial economic profit.

Finally, Putin-era alliances with African states are characterised by several alarming features, including alleged human rights violations, targeted killings and sexual assaults. Instances of extreme violence against opponents, whistleblowers and journalists have been reported, notably in Sudan, where several local journalism networks working for Western investigative outlets have faced threats of assassination, forcing them into exile. The danger of expressing dissent was tragically exemplified by the deliberate targeting of prominent pro-democracy activists during demonstrations, resulting in the deaths of ten protesters.[43] In the CAR, three Russian journalists were reportedly killed while investigating a story related to the Wagner Network.[44] Moreover, allegations of human rights abuses have emerged in Mali, with an estimated 300 deaths linked to Moscow's MSI assistance.[45] These concerning reports underscore the need for a critical examination of the impact of Moscow's secret army on human rights and security dynamics in African nations.

Overall, since Putin's third term in office, Russia has been systematically crossing Cold War red lines pertinent to its engagement in Africa. It has set up a network of crypto-state companies that enable it to operate in a deniable way. It uses its mercenaries to carry out a hybrid mix of activities aimed at state capture. And it has actively engaged in combat on behalf of some of the continent's most controversial regimes. These Faustian bargains will likely have long-term consequences not only for the populations of the African states involved, but also for the way wars will be fought in the future – how hostile and competitor states will employ commercial entities for offensive and deniable military operations. This raises critical considerations for international security and prompts an examination of the evolving landscape of hybrid warfare, where non-state actors and private entities may play increasingly prominent roles in military operations. Understanding the motivations, tactics and potential countermeasures in this context is crucial for policymakers, intelligence agencies and military strategists in developing comprehensive approaches to address the evolving nature of threats in the contemporary security environment.[46]

1. Tim Lister, Sebastian Shukla and Clarissa Ward. Putin's private army. CNN, 2019, https:edition.cnn.com/interactive/2019/08/africa/putins-private-army-car-intl/.

2. John A Lechner and Sergey Eledinov. Is Africa Corps a rebranded Wagner Group? *Foreign Policy*, 7 February 2024, https:foreignpolicy.com/2024/02/07/africa-corps-wagner-group-russia-africa-burkina-faso/.

3. For a classic on Global South interventions see Arne Westad, *The Global Cold War: Third World Interventions and the Making of Our Times*. Cambridge: Cambridge University Press, 2007. For in-depth case studies of Soviet Bloc MSI engagement see Jeffrey A Lefebvre, The United States, Ethiopia and the 1963 Somali–Soviet arms deal: containment and the balance of power dilemma in the Horn of Africa. *Journal of Modern African Studies*, vol 36, no 4, 1998; Jocelyn Alexander and JoAnn McGregor, African soldiers in the USSR: oral histories of ZAPU intelligence cadres' Soviet training, 1964–1979. *Journal of Southern African Studies*, vol 43, no 1, 2017, pp. 49–66; see articles in Special Issue: Daniela Richterova and Natalia Telepneva, An introduction: the secret struggle for the Global South – espionage, military assistance and state security in the Cold War. *International History Review*, vol 43, no 1, 2021, pp. 1–11; Natalia Telepneva, *Cold War Liberation: the Soviet Union and the Collapse of the Portuguese Empire in Africa*, 1961–1975. Chapel Hill: University of North Carolina Press, 2022; Daniela Richterova, *Watching the Jackals*. Washington DC: Georgetown University Press, 2024, ch 1.

4. Galia Golan. *The Soviet Union and National Liberation Movements in the Third World*. London: Routledge, 1988, p. 1.

5. Other institutions were also set up; see Telepneva, *Cold War Liberation*.

6. Westad, *The Global Cold War*, pp. 58, 67–8.

7. Czechoslovakia: Daniela Richterova, Mikuláš Pešta and Natalia Telepneva. Banking on military assistance: Czechoslovakia's struggle for influence and profit in the Third World 1955–1968. *International History Review*, vol 43, no 1, 2021, pp. 90–108. German Democratic Republic: Jude Howell. The end of an era: the rise and fall of GDR aid. *Journal of Modern African Studies*, vol 32, no 2, 1994, p. 312. Poland: Philip Muehlenbeck and Natalia Telepneva (eds.). *Warsaw Pact Intervention in the 'Global South': Aid and Influence in the Cold War*. London: I.B. Tauris, 2018.

8. Jeremy Friedman. *Shadow Cold War: the Sino-Soviet Competition for the Global South*. Chapel Hill: University of North Carolina Press, 2015.

9. How this shift occurred in Czechoslovakia: Richterova, Pešta and Telepneva. Banking on military assistance; Samuel Ramani. *Russia in Africa: Resurgent Great Power or Bellicose Pretender?* London: Hurst & Company, 2023, p. 16.

10. Oleg Yegorov. How the USSR fell in love with Africa. Russia Beyond, 6 November 2019, https:www.rbth.com/history/331238-ussr-africa-relations-friendship.

11. Sergey V Mazov. The Soviet Union and the Nigerian Civil War (1967–1970): military and technical co-operation with the Federal Military Government of Nigeria, in Chris Saunders, Helder Adegar Fonseca and Lena Dallywater (eds.). *Eastern Europe, the Soviet Union, and Africa: New Perspectives on the Era of Decolonization, 1950s to 1990s*. Munich, Boston: De Gruyter Oldenbourg, 2023.

12. Constantin Katsakioris. The Lumumba University in Moscow: higher education for a Soviet–Global South alliance, 1960–91. *Journal of Global History*, vol 14, no 2, 2019, pp. 281–300; Golan, *Soviet Union and National Liberation Movements*, pp. 3, 268.
13. Ramani, *Russia in Africa*, pp. 13, 15.
14. Yegorov, How the USSR fell in love with Africa.
15. Richterova, Pešta and Telepneva, Banking on military assistance, p. 94.
16. Mark Kramer. The role of the CPSU International Department in Soviet foreign relations and national security policy. *Soviet Studies*, vol 42, no 3, July 1990, pp. 429–46.
17. Motti Golani. The historical place of the Czech–Egyptian arms deal, fall 1955. *Middle Eastern Studies*, vol 31, no 4, 1995, pp. 803–27; Guy Laron. 'Logic dictates that they may attack when they feel they can win': the 1955 Czech–Egyptian arms deal, the Egyptian army, and Israeli intelligence. *Middle East Journal*, vol 63, no 1, winter 2009, pp. 69–84. On controversy about Czechoslovakia's agency in this deal, see P Zídek and K Sieber, *Československo a Blízký východ v letech* 1948–1989. Prague: Ústav mezinárodních vztahů, 2009; Philip Muehlenbeck, *Czechoslovakia in Africa, 1945–1968*. Basingstoke: Palgrave Macmillan, 2015.
18. Telepneva, *Cold War Liberation*, p. 103. Also see Alexander and McGregor, African soldiers in the USSR, pp. 49–66.
19. Howell, The end of an era, p. 312.
20. On training African revolutionaries, see Richterova, *Watching the Jackals*.
21. Egypt–Israel war of attrition: Roger E Kanet. The superpower quest for Empire: the Cold War and Soviet support for 'wars of national liberation'. *Cold War History*, vol 6, no 3, 2006, pp. 331–52. During national liberation struggles: Natalia Telepneva. Code name SEKRETÁŘ: Amílcar Cabral, Czechoslovakia and the role of human intelligence during the Cold War. *International History Review*, vol 42, no 6, 2020, pp. 13–14.
22. Yegorov, How the USSR fell in love with Africa. This was, however, not the case when it came to Moscow's most adventurous ally, Cuba. On Castro's direct engagement in African conflicts see, for instance, Frank Villafaña, *Cold War in the Congo: the Confrontation of Cuban Military Forces, 1960–1967*. London: Taylor and Francis, 2017.
23. For more of why Moscow divested in relations with Africa in the early 1990s and then revitalised them under Yevgeny Primakov, see Ramani, *Russia in Africa*, pp. 25–52.
24. See ibid for an in-depth overview of these alliances, pp. 52–104.
25. Ibid, p. 108.
26. Ibid, pp. 109–10.
27. Lister, Shukla and Ward, Putin's private army.
28. Paul Martial. Putin transforms Wagner in Africa. *International Viewpoint*, 22 December 2023, https:internationalviewpoint.org/spip.php?article8358.
29. Joseph Siegle. Russia's strategic goals in Africa. Africa Centre for Strategic Studies, 6 May 2021, https:africacenter.org/experts/joseph-siegle/russia-strategic-goals-africa/#_ednref.1.

30. Evidence of Russia-linked companies operating in these countries: ibid.
31. Written submission on Wagner's activities in Libya submitted by [organisation name redacted] (WGN0014), Foreign Affairs Committee, UK Parliament, May 2022, https:committees.parliament.uk/writtenevidence/108429/html/.
32. Guns for gold: the Wagner Network exposed. Foreign Affairs Committee, 26 July 2023, https:publications.parliament.uk/pa/cm5803/cmselect/cmfaff/167/report. html#footnote-306-backlink.
33. Written submission on Wagner's activities.
34. Richard Engel. Blood and gold: Wagner's rise in Central Africa. NBC News, 4 August 2023, https:www.youtube.com/watch?v=5sDQAW_VGg0.
35. Nima Elbagir et al. Russia is plundering gold in Sudan to boost Putin's war effort in Ukraine. CNN, 29 July 2022, https:edition.cnn.com/2022/07/29/africa/sudan-russia-gold-investigation-cmd-intl/ index.html; US pressures allies to expel Russia's Wagner mercenaries from Libya, Sudan. France 24, 3 February 2023, https:www.france24.com/en/africa/20230203-us-pressures-allies-to-expel-wagner-russian-mercenaries-from-libya-sudan.
36. Todd Prince. Expansion or contraction? How Putin's war in Ukraine affects his efforts in Africa. Radio Free Europe/Radio Liberty, 24 May 2022, https:www.rferl.org/a/russia-africa-ukraine-war-impact/31865709.html.
37. Training army recruits in the CAR: Lister, Shukla and Ward, Putin's private army. Training in Sudan: US pressures allies, France 24.
38. US pressures allies, France 24.
39. Written submission on Wagner's activities.
40. Lister, Shukla and Ward, Putin's private army.
41. US pressures allies, France 24; Guns for gold; Written submission on Wagner's activities.
42. In October 2021, a month after the anti-corruption committee stopped the transfer of holdings from Meroe Gold to al-Solag, Sudan's military staged a coup – which US official and former official sources accuse Russia of backing – and the junta immediately dismantled the committee. Elbagir et al, Russia is plundering gold in Sudan.
43. Ibid.
44. Tim Lister, Mary Ilyushina and Sebastian Shukla. Murdered chasing mercenaries. CNN, 4 August 2018, https:edition.cnn.com/2018/08/04/africa/russia-journal-ists-car-intl/index.html.
45. Russian mercenaries behind Central African Republic atrocities – HRW. BBC News, 3 May 2022, https:www.bbc.co.uk/news/world-africa-61311272.
46. Guns for gold.

COMMUNICATION
AND CONTEMPORARY
CONFLICT

A Russian signal corps serviceman
uses an Azart radio station at an
unknown location in Russia, 2023.

TACTICAL COMMUNICATIONS AND SECRECY IN CONTEMPORARY CONFLICT: HISTORICAL AND TECHNOLOGICAL PERSPECTIVES

Tony Ingesson

In the first few days of fighting following the full-scale Russian invasion of Ukraine in February 2022, Russian troops suddenly found themselves without a reliable means of communication. The encrypted mobile phones they had invested in so heavily were not working, and the much-hyped modern Russian field radios were in short supply. To remedy these shortcomings, desperate Russian commanders started using various improvised solutions. Those who resorted to civilian mobiles or insecure radios were easily intercepted and localised by the Ukrainians. In many cases, the contents of their communications traffic were analysed for intelligence purposes, while in other examples snipers were sent to the source of the transmission to target senior Russian commanders.[1] In addition, civilian radios are rarely designed to cope with electronic warfare, making them vulnerable to jamming, which the Ukrainians were quick to exploit.[2]

This spectacular failure illustrates two arguably timeless aspects of battlefield communications, which we can call *the command dimension* and *the secrecy dimension*. In terms of the command dimension, any communications system will to varying extents *enable* and simultaneously *constrain* the actions of those using it. Secrecy, on the other hand, presents both an *opportunity* and a possible *vulnerability*. Using these two concept pairs, I will discuss how they can help us understand the role of communications on the battlefield. However, to illustrate these concepts, we need a bit of historical and technical background, starting with the former.

The first thing we must note is that for thousands of years, military command on the battlefield was limited to the distance a voice could carry, a bugle be heard, or a signal flag seen. The men fighting at Hastings in 1066 would have recognised the methods of communication employed almost 600 years later at Breitenfeld.[3] A sophisticated commander could use messengers to direct a larger force over some distance, but the ancient limits were still making themselves felt.[4]

It is thus impossible to overstate how revolutionary the telegraph was when it was introduced. Optical semaphore telegraphs were already around in the early 1800s, comprising tall poles with signal flags. These would then mirror each other to 'transmit' messages across vast distances. However, the speed was slow and it could only be used when visibility was relatively good.[5] Thus, when Samuel Morse and Alfred Vail developed the modern telegraph in the 1830s and 1840s, they revolutionised communications by allowing human interaction to transcend the boundaries of physical distance. By the mid-1850s, the most important European cities were already linked by telegraph wires, while military organisations like the Prussian army's telegraphic institute were scrambling to adopt the new technology.[6] In these early days of the telegraph, it was primarily useful as a means to facilitate mobilisation, deployment and communications between the armies and their headquarters in the rear.[7] In this capacity, the telegraph was a key *enabler*, making it possible to coordinate troop movements and create complex logistics schedules.

As early as 1859, senior officers were starting to notice that the telegraph was also imposing limits on their autonomy, by enabling detailed control over subordinate formations across vast distances.[8] This illustrates the *constraining* aspect of the command dimension. The use of the telegraph enabled a hitherto unseen degree of micromanagement on behalf of central decision-makers, thus adding a new constraint that had previously been absent. The telegraph was, however, always limited by the physical nature of the wires it depended on. Poles had to be erected and spools of wire carried, in addition to the time it took to build the physical foundations for this infrastructure. Furthermore, as would become evident once again during the First World War, telegraph wires were highly vulnerable to artillery fire as well as sabotage.[9]

In the last years of the 1800s, the next major revolution in military communications arrived in the form of 'wireless', also known as radio. The pioneer most often associated with this breakthrough is Guglielmo Marconi, who built on experiments carried out by Oliver Lodge and Heinrich Hertz to construct a functional communications system.[10] In the summer of 1895, the first experimental wireless transmission signalled the birth of a new era. No more than four years later, the Royal Navy was using the new system during manoeuvres, linking ships at a distance of 150 kilometres. Being able to communicate beyond visual distance, even beyond the curvature of the earth, opened up new possibilities for naval operations (*enabling* new tactical and operational approaches).

The physical nature of wireless systems made them uniquely suitable for naval purposes, since seawater provided an excellent opportunity to *ground* the equipment. For this reason, naval forces and civilian shipping were much faster to adopt wireless technology than their land-based counterparts. The explanation for why this was the case requires a bit of technical background.

First of all, some antennas require good grounding – a good connection to the earth – to work properly. This has to do with the physics of radio reception and transmission. A radio signal, which typically travels at the speed of light (300,000 kilometres per second) can be described using either wavelength, ie the physical distance between the peaks of the electromagnetic wave carrying the transmission, commonly measured in metres, or frequency, ie the number of cycles per second of the wave, measured in hertz (see *Figure 1*).

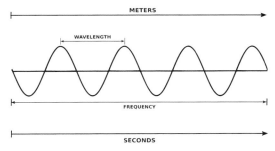

Figure 1: Wavelength and frequency

Most antennas are based on the *resonance principle*, which means there is a direct relationship between the length of the antenna and the wavelength it is best suited to receive. As a simplified rule of thumb, an antenna is often said to be *resonant* with a radio signal when it is of the same physical length as the wavelength of the transmission. An antenna whose length matches the wavelength is also referred to as a full-wave antenna. However, a full-wave antenna was often impractical in the early 20th century, since wireless communications then tended to use fairly long wavelengths. For example, during the First World War, a typical Marconi wireless set used wavelengths between 300 and 1000 metres (700 metres was the usual operational value).[11]

Another option is to make the antenna resonant at a specific fraction of the wavelength. Typical designs include half-wave (half the wavelength) and quarter-wave (a quarter of the wavelength) antennas. For example, for the 80-metre band (3.5–4 megahertz – MHz – ie 3.5–4 million cycles per second in terms of frequency), a quarter-wave antenna needs to be about 20 metres long. Modern radio systems where the frequencies are in the thousands of MHz, such as Wi-Fi (typically 2.4 GHz–5 GHz, equating to 2,400 MHz–5,000 MHz), consequently have much shorter wavelengths, a mere 12 centimetres for 2.4 GHz, meaning an antenna can be very short, albeit at the expense of range. Some more traditional radio transmissions that are still in use, such as the FM radio many still listen to while driving, have a wavelength of around three metres.

The extent to which a ground connection is needed, if at all, is also related to antenna length and wavelength (where longer wavelengths require more grounding). A half-wave antenna only needs a modestly effective connection to the earth, but if we move on to a quarter-wave antenna in combination with long wavelengths, the ground connection needs to have very low electrical resistance to work properly – otherwise the energy used to transmit ends up heating the ground rather than going through the antenna.[12] The ability to establish a good electrical connection to ground depends largely on how conductive the connection is. Moist earth, for example, conducts electricity far more effectively than dry sand. Water, as most of us know, conducts electricity well, and the more salty the water is, the better it conducts (this is why seawater is particularly suited for grounding). Thus, grounding a radio set on board a ship was significantly easier than for units operating on land. Ships, with their elevated superstructures, were also suitable for masts and other solutions for raising the antennas high above sea level, improving reception and transmission conditions. The long wavelengths used during the early days of radio also necessitated very long antennas, which were relatively easy to rig on ships compared to how ground units on the move constantly had to go through the process of setting up and dismantling unwieldy installations.

Even though wireless communications had been employed in a limited scale during the Boer War, the Russo-Japanese War of 1904–5 and the Balkan War of 1912, not everyone had realised the potential this technology offered. The dry conditions during the Boer War frustrated British efforts to use wireless in support of ground operations, because of the difficulty in achieving good grounding. Thus the British army failed to see the full potential of wireless technology and entered the First World War woefully unprepared, with less wireless equipment than the Romanian army had deployed during the Balkan War two years earlier.[13] During the course of the war, both the British and the Germans made good use of wire-bound communications, establishing extensive networks, protected from shellfire, with redundant connections.[14] However, as soon as the troops advanced away from their fixed positions and into no man's land, they moved out of command range.[15]

The Royal Navy had been much more enthusiastic about wireless technology, placing an order for no less than 26 sets as early as July 1900.[16] On the other side of the Atlantic, the United States army was experimenting with radios in combat conditions in Cuba and the Philippines in the early 1900s.[17] This included Morse signalling, which, although initially associated with wire-bound telegraphy, turned out to be even more useful in conjunction with radio. This can be explained by looking at the technical specifics of how Morse works. Morse is transmitted over radio using something known as continuous wave (CW). In essence, CW is to this day still one of the most effective ways imaginable of conveying information via radio, because of two factors: it needs only a very narrow bandwidth; and it can be used even in the most challenging reception conditions. This is in part because Morse is binary (it only needs to convey two types of simple signal, the short 'dits' and the longer 'dahs'). The low transmission rate of Morse means it can be relayed using an extremely narrow bandwidth, in the order of 100–150 hertz. This can be compared to voice communications, which require circa 2,500–3000 hertz (see *Figure 2*).

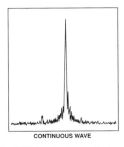 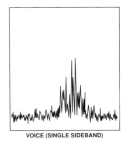

CONTINUOUS WAVE   VOICE (SINGLE SIDEBAND)

Figure 2: Bandwidth of CW and voice radio transmissions

This limited bandwidth means CW is less affected by various kinds of interference, since very narrow filters can be used on the receiving side to remove interference and noise, thus making it more effective.

The second part of the explanation is related to the decoding of the signal, which is done by the human brain rather than a machine. The advantage of this is that the human brain can be trained to a high degree of skill in filtering out noise and even intuitively to correct errors and fill in blanks, enabling effective communications even when reception conditions are poor. The rhythmic nature of Morse, more akin to music than data transmissions, is perfectly suited to the particular human capabilities also associated with our ability to listen to music and play instruments. For these reasons, Morse persisted for a long time in radio communications – and is still used today, as we shall discuss in more detail later.

First, however, we will return to the end of the First World War, when wireless had proven itself as a technology not only at sea but also as an indispensable tool for land warfare. Rather than suffering heavy casualties trying to repair telephone and telegraph wires during artillery bombardments, messages could be safely transmitted using radios. The technology had also been subject to rapid development. Starting with the cumbersome Marconi sets carried on horse-drawn carts, the war saw the creation of the compact BF (British Field) Trench Set, which fitted into a wooden box that could be carried by a single man, although it still weighed 14 kilograms.[18] This represents another key advance in *enabling* the rapid and easy deployment of command and control functions (as opposed to having to move multiple heavy vehicles in order to set up a command post with a wireless connection).

During the interwar years, the technology that had been cutting edge during the First World War was implemented on a larger scale. Germany in particular adopted radios as a means to enable fast-moving units to stay in contact with each other. Heinz Guderian, one of the creators of the modern Panzer divisions, had been a Signals and General Staff officer during the First World War, and was well aware of the potential in radios.[19] During the Second World War, radios became truly ubiquitous and were seen as essential tools for infantry, ground vehicles, aircraft, ships and submarines. The new forms of tactical sophistication seen during the war, ranging from combined arms warfare to coordinated submarine attacks and close air support, were in many cases enabled by the proliferation of radios.

During the Cold War, radios became increasingly portable and able to make more efficient use of battery power, first thanks to the miniaturisation of valves (such as in the AN/PRC-10 used by American troops in the

Korean War) and later because solid-state components started to replace valves altogether. As part of the latter development, the AN/PRC-77 fielded during the Vietnam War represented a major step, being an all-solid-state radio. Even with these technological breakthroughs, the challenges of physics remained the same in some areas, such as the struggle to properly ground antennas used for long-range communications in Vietnam.[20] American military advisers in Vietnam in the years before the war also complained of being deprived of their autonomy when the communications infrastructure there was expanded, echoing the sentiments expressed by their predecessors in the 19th century when the telegraph was introduced.[21] After the Cold War, tactical radios continued to develop to incorporate software-defined radio (SDR) and advanced networking and information-sharing capabilities.[22]

While the evolution of radio has resulted in increasingly indispensable tools for coordination and command, there is also a downside to wireless communications: the signals transmitted are much easier to intercept than those travelling through wires. This kind of interception, today included under the wide umbrella of signals intelligence (SIGINT), was used as early as the Russo-Japanese War, when French intelligence set up a radio intercept station at the top of the Eiffel Tower to listen in on the messages sent by the Japanese ambassador to Paris.[23] In the years that followed there was a growing realisation of the importance of protecting these signals. This resulted in the creation of portable but efficient encryption devices, such as the infamous German Enigma machines. However, the Germans vastly underrated the ability of their adversaries to break this new kind of machine encryption. As a result, British codebreakers, building on the work started by their Polish counterparts, were able to build efficient code-breaking devices, known as *bombes*.[24] This sped up the process and enabled the timely handling of larger volumes of communications traffic.

This development illustrates the second dimension: *secrecy*. The growing capacity to intercept enemy signals presented a vulnerability the Germans were well aware of, since they had been intercepting signals as far back as the early years of the First World War. Thus, the Enigma and other encryption devices were developed to reduce this vulnerability. At the same time, the shortcomings of German encryption technology presented an opportunity for the Allies, who could gain invaluable insights into German plans and movements. Meanwhile, in the Pacific, Indigenous American radio operators had used their native Navajo language as a

US Marine Corporal Lloyd Oliver
operating a field radio in the South
Pacific during the Second World War.

simple but effective form of encryption for tactical communications. Later, during the Cold War, technology enabled the use of portable encryption devices such as the KY-38, which was compatible with the previously mentioned PRC-77.[25]

In the jungles of Vietnam, new systems had to be developed to cope with the challenges of that particular environment and context. This included specialised systems for relaying information across vast distances using high-powered so-called 'troposcatter' systems, as well as the new ARC-44 FM radio for air-to-ground coordination. Before the ARC-44 became widespread, forward air controllers in spotter planes had to use two separate radios, one for a high range of the Very High Frequency spectrum for talking to the air force aircraft and one with a lower range (an infantryman's PRC-10 strapped to a chair in the plane) for talking to the ground units.[26]

As shown in the historical examples presented above, tactical communications technology both enables and constrains armies in the field. It enables command to be exercised more efficiently, as well as across distances. In this sense, it also enables rapid movements of military units, while still maintaining coordination. At the same time, communications technology constrains. On the one hand, it can limit the autonomy of subordinate commanders. On the other, the practical range of the communications technology used may become a limit for advancing troops, as seen during the First World War. Equipment that takes time to set up will impose time constraints, forcing units to halt in order to re-establish communications. In the same manner, heavy and cumbersome equipment will require vehicles or pack animals, which in turn may not be able to cross the same ground as the troops, forcing the units to stick to more passable terrain if they need to maintain contact with the wireless operators.

The ability to protect the contents of what is being communicated is crucial, as are efforts to break the signals protection used by the adversary. Being able to read encrypted communications, without the other party realising it, can be an exceptionally powerful force multiplier. Thus, secrecy presents another theoretical dimension, which concerns vulnerability and opportunity. On the one hand, failures to uphold secrecy will quickly become a vulnerability, while on the other hand, if you can listen in on the adversary's communications, this represents a tremendous opportunity.

	Negative aspects	Positive aspects
Secrecy dimension	Vulnerability	Opportunity
Command dimension	Constraining	Enabling

Table 1: Negative and positive aspects of the dimensions

Returning to the full-scale Russian invasion of Ukraine in 2022, we can see that during the first critical days and weeks, Russian forces found themselves struggling to communicate. Numerous pictures and reports were emerging showing Russian troops using civilian radios, such as Baofeng UV-5R and UV-82.[27]

Russian battlefield communications were also making use of insecure HF (High Frequency, ie 3–30 MHz) transmissions. Despite its traditional name, HF is by contemporary standards low on the frequency spectrum, since technological development has since produced new devices capable of using higher frequencies, forcing the International Telecommunication Union (ITU) to propose increasingly strained prefixes. This includes VHF (Very High Frequency, 30–300 MHz), UHF (Ultra High Frequency, 300MHz–3 GHz) and SHF (Super High Frequency, 3–30 GHz). HF has been a Russian preference for some time, since although it is associated with older technology, it is still a robust means of communication. Signals can be bounced off the ionosphere (in the upper parts of the atmosphere, at an altitude of 50 to 2,000 kilometres) to achieve significant range.[28] Somewhat ironically, older analogue systems may sometimes be more difficult to jam than more modern digital ones, since only about one-third of a digital signal needs to be disrupted to render the transmission useless (unless it includes measures to make jamming more difficult, such as error correction), whereas an analogue signal requires more extensive jamming, due to the human brain's ability to anticipate and compensate for information loss in a signal.[29] However, the lack of encryption in the Russian transmissions is somewhat puzzling. Possible explanations include that the units had not been issued encryption equipment for their radios, or that these devices were not working as intended.[30]

One aspect of contemporary Russian communications that may seem puzzling to the uninitiated, but which can be understood through the earlier technical explanation, is the continued Russian reliance on Morse radio-telegraphy. Combining Morse with HF radio offers a very affordable and effective long-range communications solution. The fact that

Russian large aircraft and ships in particular make use of this technology can be understood in technical terms: they are still subject to the same physics as their predecessors nearly a hundred years ago. Antennas still need to be a certain length to be effective on low frequencies, which makes large planes and ships particularly suited as platforms. While it may seem counterintuitive, large aircraft can also easily provide good grounding by making use of the aircraft body and static wicks (the small antenna-like protrusions on the aft of the wings often seen on large aircraft, including airliners) to dissipate excess electricity into the atmosphere.[31]

One downside is that many of these Morse transmissions are unencrypted and can be easily intercepted even by amateur radio enthusiasts. There are for example several accounts on X (formerly Twitter) reporting on both Russian naval and air units (such as the strategic bombers) based on their transmissions.

If we apply the previously presented theoretical perspective, the Russian communications failures in Ukraine can be understood as a maximisation of the negative aspects while at the same time featuring an inability to leverage any of the positive aspects. Meanwhile, the Ukrainian defenders as well as third parties assisting them have successfully exploited the opportunities provided by the Russian vulnerability. More specifically, the Russians failed to enable their units to use communications efficiently on the battlefield. Thus, they were constrained by the absence of a communications infrastructure they had become dependent upon. Their attempts at improvising by using insecure civilian equipment instead may to some extent have reduced that constraint and instead acted as an enabler (albeit less effectively than more specialised equipment), but on the other hand, the lack of security maximised their vulnerability by both making the contents of the transmissions available and inviting localisation and jamming.

In an echo of the issues American troops in Vietnam struggled with, not only Russian ground forces but also Russian pilots in Ukraine have been observed carrying civilian radios in numerous photos from the conflict.[32] Since Russian aircraft are no doubt equipped with working radios for contacting other aircraft and air traffic control (otherwise even peacetime flight operations would be nearly impossible; even under optimal conditions, obtaining clearance for landing and take-off are a necessity to run an airfield), these radios are most likely intended for coordinating with ground units. The improvised nature of this arrangement resembles the use of strapped-in PRC-10s by forward air controllers over Vietnam, as described above. It also shows that having communications equipment is not by itself enough; compatibility has to be ensured through long-term planning and preparation.

From a theoretical point of view this is particularly interesting, since it represents a significant degree of failure in both negative dimensions while at the same time achieving minimal advantages on the positive side. In most conflicts, including those discussed above, there is more of a balance. For example, during the First and Second World Wars, security was a major issue (vulnerability), but at the same time this was to some extent offset by the increase in command ability (enabling). This double negative of both vulnerability and constraint was arguably a key element in the overall Russian command failure, resulting in a sharp drop in tempo/movement as units had to halt to establish communications, as well as a significant degradation in their ability to coordinate.

In the second year of fighting, Russian forces were still heavily reliant on unencrypted analogue radio communications from the battalion level down. According to a Royal United Services Institute report, this may be the result of shortcomings in training.[33] Reconnaissance units and artillery observers, however, have access to more secure alternatives. It should also be noted that the Russians are showing clear signs of adaptation, which can be expected to improve their performance. For example, while Russian electronic warfare systems were widely seen as not living up to the expectations from before the war during the first months, the continued fighting in Ukraine has seen these platforms being used in a more efficient manner. On the one hand, they are used to inflict relatively heavy casualties on Ukrainian drones, while on the other they are allegedly used to intercept and decrypt Motorola 256-bit encrypted tactical communications (which are widely employed by the Ukrainian armed forces).[34]

Thus, while the pattern seen in the first year after the full-scale Russian invasion of Ukraine may be unusual in terms of the severity of the communications failure, the pattern of adaptation and improvement is more familiar. By viewing the war in Ukraine through both a historical and technological lens, the role and importance of tactical communications can be more readily understood. As the conflict continues to unfold, we can expect the interplay between command and secrecy, as well as the inescapable limitations imposed by physics, to remain as relevant as they ever were.

1. Jack Detsch and Amy Mackinnon. The Ukrainians are listening: Russia's military radios are getting owned. *Foreign Policy*, 22 March 2022, https:foreignpolicy.com/2022/03/22/ukraine-russia-military-radio/.
2. Why Russian radios in Ukraine are getting spammed with heavy metal. *The Economist*, 28 March 2022, https:www.economist.com/the-economist-explains/2022/03/28/why-russian-radios-ukraine-war-intercepted-heavy-metal.
3. Martin Van Creveld. *Command in War.* Cambridge, MA: Harvard University Press, 1985, pp. 50–1.
4. Ibid, p. 54.
5. Chris Rutkowski. *The CW Way of Life: Learning, Living, and Loving Morse Code (in a Digital World).* MorseBusters Publishing, p. 22.
6. Van Creveld, *Command,* p. 107.
7. Ibid, p. 109.
8. Ibid, p. 108.
9. Peter R Jensen. *Wireless at War: Developments in Military and Clandestine Radio, 1895–2012.* Kenthurst: Rosenberg, 2013, p. 55.
10. Ibid, p. 12.
11. Ibid, p. 58.
12. National Association for Amateur Radio, Grounding, https:www.arrl.org/grounding.
13. Jensen, *Wireless,* p. 38.
14. Simon Godfrey. *British Army Communications in the Second World War: Lifting the Fog of Battle.* London: Bloomsbury, 2013, p. 15.
15. Ibid.
16. Jensen, *Wireless,* p. 34.
17. William R Blair. Army radio in war and peace. *Annals of the American Academy of Political and Social Science,* vol 142, no 1, 1929, pp. 86–9.
18. Jensen, *Wireless,* p. 71.
19. Ibid, p. 119.
20. John D Bergen. *Military Communications: a Test For Technology.* Washington DC: Center of Military History, United States Army, 1986, p. 74.
21. Ibid, p. 54.
22. See for example the SYNAPS family produced by Thales: https:www.thalesgroup.com/en/markets/defence-and-security/radio-communications/synaps/full-product-range-highly-scalable.
23. Roger Faligot, France, Sigint and the Cold War. *Intelligence & National Security,* vol 16, no 1, 2001, pp. 177–8.
24. Clay Blair. *Hitlers ubåtskrig,* vol 1: *Vargar på jakt 1941–1942.* Stockholm: Hjalmarson & Högberg Bokförlag, 2004, pp. 344–5.
25. Jensen, *Wireless,* p. 219.
26. Bergen, *Communications,* p. 57.
27. Sam Cranny-Evans and Thomas Withington. Russian comms in Ukraine: a world of hertz. Royal United Services Institute, 9 March 2022, https:rusi.org/explore-our-research/publications/commentary/russian-comms-ukraine-world-hertz.

28. John S Seybold. *Introduction to RF Propagation*. Hoboken, NJ: John Wiley & Sons, 2005, p. 7.

29. David L Adamy. *EW 103: Tactical Battlefield Communications Electronic Warfare*. Boston: Artech House, 2008, p. 257.

30. Cranny-Evans and Withington, Russian comms.

31. How are airplanes electrically grounded? Monroe Aerospace, 2009, https:monroe-aerospace.com/blog/how-are-airplanes-electrically-grounded/.

32. See for example https:x.com/RALee85/status/1532844928434327553?s=20 or https:x.com/ItsArtoir/status/1545835056484204545?s=20.

33. Jack Watling and Nick Reynolds. Meatgrinder: Russian tactics in the second year of its invasion of Ukraine. Special Report, Royal United Services Institute for Defence and Security Studies, 19 May 2023, p. 24.

34. Ibid, p. iii.

A young woman films a destroyed
shopping centre after a Russian shelling
attack in Kyiv,Ukraine, March 2022.

WAR IN THE AGE OF THE SMARTPHONE: UKRAINE AND CONTEMPORARY CONFLICT

Matthew Ford

Our capacity to know and understand war depends on a range of media ecosystems that work differently in different parts of the world. In Ethiopia, Myanmar and Kazakhstan, governments engaged in security crackdowns, genocide or war have been active in shutting down the web or controlling access to online media.[1] This has had distorting effects on how political violence has come to be represented and understood in social and mainstream media (MSM). During the last decade this has not been obvious to audiences in Europe or North America. However, Russia's 2022 invasion of Ukraine has started to bring home the realities of war in a way not previously experienced in the West. The principal device for bringing these images to our attention is the smartphone.

In this short essay I argue that the smartphone now plays a fundamental role in shaping both how war is represented and how it is conducted.[2] The war in Ukraine is the most connected conventional conflict in history, and the smartphone is the unifying central experience for people, whether they are directing kinetic activity on the battlefield or watching the war while sitting on public transport in another part of the world. War in these new digital contexts is participative in ways that have never previously been possible.[3]

The smartphone offers a window onto contemporary conflict. With one device you can access the government, amplify the war, kill the enemy, donate to crowdfunding campaigns, watch a movie and talk to your family at home while sitting in a trench at the front.[4] For civilians, the smartphone enables people in a conflict to monitor events and for refugees beyond the war zone to maintain contact with their homeland. In effect the device is helping to collapse the frontline and the home front into one deeply mediatised experience.[5]

In the case of Ukraine, the government is now accessible via cloud services.[6] Accessing the internet is a critical infrastructure for everyone, irrespective of whether they are on the battlefield or trying to work from home. Russian efforts to switch it off have degraded access to the internet but not prevented people from getting online. Ukraine's telecoms engineers are in a battle to keep 4G networks running even as Russia's hackers try to steal Ukrainian personal data.

When it comes to the conduct of war, soldiers use phones as controllers for their drones, helping them to adjust artillery fire onto targets. Ukrainians caught up in the occupation zones risk taking photographs of enemy movements.[7] Social media influencers use them to spread 'warnography' and disinformation. Handheld smart devices provide the technology platform for battlefield target identification, coordination and prioritisation software. Energy grids and electricity supply are limited. This forces a critical choice upon soldiers and civilians alike: turn on the lights or power up the smartphone?

At the same time, the smartphone democratises the public's engagement with war. There is an army of data scientists working to hoover up vast quantities of data in the hope that they might help the armed forces render the battlefield transparent.[8] Backed by Silicon Valley, these analysts claim to have a privileged, bird's-eye view of wars in different parts of the world. Their ambition is to optimise killing by speeding up the process of target acquisition through data collection and processing. But their engagement with war is asymmetrical to the smartphone-wielding public, who are overwhelmed by an explosion of information but lack the means to make sense of it. This asymmetry needs further exploration, because it reflects a much deeper politics that leaves both soldiers and civilians as mere data points in the machinations of the software engineer.

The information space relating to the war in Ukraine, for example, is complex and is both hyperlocal and global. In the first instance the means for producing, publishing and consuming the war exists in the form of the smartphone.[9] Supporting this technology is a series of interlocking systems that reveal that Ukraine has a highly connected information ecosystem. For example, before the 2022 invasion, the International Telecommunication Union, an agency of the United Nations, reported that 79% of Ukrainian households have access to the internet at home, 85% of inhabitants have active mobile broadband subscriptions, 89% of the

Kyiv residents charge their mobile phones
at a 'Point of Invincibility' during a power
outage caused by a Russian rocket attack,
December 2022.

population have a mobile phone, and 87% of the population is covered by at least a 4G network.[10] Since the beginning of the full-scale invasion, this information grid has been subject to a great deal of enemy action. As a result, Ukraine's information infrastructure is in a constant state of flux as it gets rebuilt and reorganised in an effort to sustain connectivity for both the armed forces and society.

Nevertheless, the smartphone represents the handheld manifestation of this sophisticated ecosystem of information infrastructure. As a device for recording the 'now', the smartphone adds geolocation to videos of events. It has limitations, if belligerents switch off the internet, but both sides recognise that the web is vital to society, government and the conduct of the war. So Russia and Ukraine try to route access to the internet through those telecoms grids they control. This facilitates the surveillance of internet users even as the internet makes possible some semblance of ordinary life in the war zone. At the same time, it enables Russia's efforts at population engineering in the occupied zones of the Donbas and beyond. The smartphone is changing events, reformatting their representation, manipulating users' thoughts and redefining how the war is being fought.

These changes reflect a new geometry of power that is transnational in nature, underpinned by information infrastructures that are rarely considered or reflected upon. This is not just a matter of Elon Musk's Starlink low orbital satellite technology that keeps Ukraine online even when its mobile phone grid shuts down but is also related to the plethora of other systems that make the internet possible. Big Tech use their capacity to algorithmically intervene to shape the representation of war. Silicon Valley companies apply artificial intelligence to help sift through the vast quantities of data produced by everyday users. Patterns are identified and people's online posts are deleted before they can be used in propaganda or to help the enemy. But this is an ongoing battle between users, social media platforms and governments. Some governments get privileged access to Big Tech. Others must watch as global corporations ignore requests while data gets leaked and produces unintended political outcomes.

Understanding the evolution of Ukraine's information stack – that unique arrangement of servers, telecoms grids, smartphones and other connected devices that frame user engagement – is important. This is because Ukraine is now using information infrastructures that stretch well beyond its borders to construct a new digital sovereignty. Prior to the 2022 invasion, Ukraine's government bureaucracy had a physical presence located in sovereign Ukrainian territory. Now their services are hosted in the cloud, citizens must go online to access the services that previously required a visit to a government office. Once controlled by employees of the state, Ukraine's future is now also bound to the internet service providers that power much of the world's networked economy. Even if Ukraine ceases to exist territorially, it will survive as a virtual space with a global diaspora around the world. The future memory of Ukraine will have a life regardless of the outcome of the war.

As a result, as anyone can work and make use of data wherever they are in the world, it is hard to define where the battlefield starts and where it ends. In this respect, this new ecology of war has not been properly quantified. Civilians from a neutral country on the other side of the planet can help with military-targeting data for Ukraine's intelligence fusion cells just as easily as can Ukrainian citizens on the frontlines. Military targeting is itself now outsourced to private companies crunching open-source information and working alongside Ukraine's armed forces.[11] This complex stack of interlocking sociotechnical systems increases the attack surfaces available for kinetic attacks and cyberattacks. Are these people or organisations legitimate targets for Russian strikes? What about the data centres and the satellites, the cellular networks and the undersea cables?

Given the ubiquity of connected devices both at and beyond the battlefield, the implication is that civilian and military information infrastructures for both information sharing and targeting are now tightly bound. Thus, successive cyberattacks by Russian military and intelligence services have sought to hack Ukrainian citizens' personal information. This might be gained from data held by insurers, telecoms companies or on social media platforms. Pre-war efforts to collate this data appear to have been designed to help the invasion forces identify potential supporters and enemies of any Russian occupation. Advance access to this information would be helpful for managing the organisation of repression once Ukraine had fallen. Mundane data provided by everyday civilian interactions with the new war ecology thus offer 'fantastically useful information if you're planning an occupation…knowing exactly which car everyone drives and where they live'.[12]

This preparation of the battlefield to identify and kill those who resist is not especially new. Genocide by smartphone has already occurred in

Myanmar, and there is plenty of evidence to suggest the same has been occurring as part of the civil war between Ethiopian government forces and rebels in Tigray.[13] Civilian smartphones are being used to create resilient kill chains that spread the intelligence collection effort out beyond the military and into civil society. At the same time, smartphone use creates exploitable data points for controlling populations and has been interpreted by Russian soldiers fighting in Ukraine as a hostile act. As a consequence, smartphone use has blurred the line between civilian and combatant.

On a battlefield, with constantly moving adversaries, a civilian-enabled sensor network powered by the smartphone creates the potential for an even more dynamic military-targeting cycle. Given the distorting effects of social media, and the sociotechnical challenge of fusing different intelligence sources, it is unlikely that targeting is now being conducted exclusively on these platforms. Instead, a combination of sources is likely to provide the necessary information to allow Ukraine's armed forces to target Russia's military. This will involve fusing different intelligence sources from allied ISTAR (intelligence, surveillance, target acquisition and reconnaissance) assets with images that have been broadcast online and via MSM, as well as information passed up from military units and civilians on the battlefield.

Involving civilians in the target acquisition cycle nevertheless exposes them to the possibility that they become legitimate targets for enemy action. Russian troops have shot Ukrainian civilians for taking pictures or filming them. Now the question is whether raising a smartphone to photograph an enemy column constitutes a hostile act. There is already video evidence online showing how people using smartphones to record Russian military activity have found themselves under fire. *Economist* reporter Tim Judah observes: 'The Russians arrested people and shot them in the street to make an example because what they were really frightened of was the Ukrainians using their phones to report to Ukrainian forces their positions.'[14]

Military commanders might choose to interpret the laws of armed conflict (LOAC) in such a way as to allow them to target civilians using their smartphones. Like the NATO attack on Serbian broadcasters in Sarajevo in 1999, they might claim that the civilians were simply in the way of a military objective. What could count against such arguments relates to the question of proportionality. If civilian losses are inevitable as a result of the dual character of the target, then the collateral damage must be balanced against the military advantage to be gained. In this circumstance, indiscriminate damage is not permissible and the attack must not cause unnecessary civilian casualties. How the LOAC will be interpreted in light of attacks on civilians using smartphones does therefore need to be contextualised by reference to this question of proportionality.

Bearing all of this in mind, what distinguishes historical precedent from current practice is the global scale of interconnectedness and the way everyday civilian technology can be put to military practice. The LOAC are not geared for participative war in this context. It is apparent that smartphones constitute the tip of a civilian information infrastructure with an almost unknowable political geography. The quantity of data produced by the stack is beyond human comprehension, and its virality is far from transparent. To mine and make sense of this material demands the application of sophisticated proprietary algorithms. This capacity is not available to everyone. The private ownership of social media platforms means they are subject to the preferences and algorithmic biases of their owners and shareholders and do not represent a global commons for the free exchange of ideas. Social media platforms themselves have the power and authority to decide what data is kept and what is pulled from sight, how data is stored and referenced or attributed with metadata.[15] The interpretation of best practice for storing this data will have a profound effect on how it is perceived, analysed and used in the future, by historians, lawyers and others. Social media standards do exist for storing data at this scale, but those standards have to be retrofitted with military-targeting and war crimes prosecutions in mind.

From the perspective of those trying to prosecute war crimes, this need to retrofit standards has been troubling.[16] The implication is that digital archives are unstable and may be edited by platform content managers even before they appear in public. This is an everyday problem for social media platforms and it has implications for how digital evidence is used to investigate war crimes. War crimes reporting in Ukraine depends on communities themselves making the initial recording of an incident. With so many Ukrainians having access to smartphones, one incident may be recorded by different people from multiple perspectives. As the investigative watchdog Airwars has found out, this creates more forensic demands on investigators. When it comes to digital media, much depends on how well trained investigators are in the use and storage of data.

This is especially important as digital data tends to corroborate physical and documentary evidence of war crimes rather than become the main evidential plank in these cases. This poses questions as to whether international war crimes courts can measure the veracity and keep up with the quantity of material likely to emerge from the war in Ukraine.

Given the length of time involved in investigating war crimes, it is also possible that public concern for breaches of the LOAC will lapse. This is partly a function of being overwhelmed by the sheer quantity of imagery that now appears online. As Steve Kostas, a lawyer with the Open Society Justice Initiative, observes, civil society groups in Ukraine, digital activists and lawyers are already thinking through how evidence is collected and maintained. Kostas writes that 'thinking about these chain of command questions, the unit location, direction of firing' is all being undertaken now by those working on Ukraine war crimes. However, he goes on to note that despite the availability of 'this sort of information in the Syrian context…nobody looked at [it] for years after the events '. [17] There is a lot of ambition to work on war crimes tribunals. At the same time, despite the abundance of evidence of atrocity in a number of wars from Syria to Yemen, little has been done to push ahead with prosecutions.

In these new conditions, Ukraine shows us that anyone can participate in war. If anyone can participate, however, then what happens to the bystanders? This question is not limited to people at home amplifying social media messages, but also includes the possibility that ordinary civilians can participate in targeting adversaries simply by processing open-source information from wherever they are in the world. Can these civilians, working outside of Ukraine, now be regarded as combatants in the same way as soldiers, just by dint of using the same software and devices? The implication then is that the differences between soldier and civilian, armed forces and society have collapsed, not just on the frontlines but everywhere a conflict is being reproduced and people engage with it. To be provocative, in this new world, you cannot be a bystander if you carry a smartphone. Now everyone is a data point on the information grid.

Inevitably, this is challenging the traditional ways of making sense of war. On the one hand a sophisticated insider community of data scientists, sometimes making use of advanced artificial intelligence, hoover up vast quantities of data which they then seek to represent in targeting dashboards designed to optimise killing. On the other, the general public are confronted by the churning conundrum of regurgitated imagery constantly being vomited up online. Thus, the culture of war under digital conditions – how we know about war, how war is organised as a social activity, and how it connects back to the traditional structures of state, society and the armed forces – requires recalibration.

The analysis set out above is not designed to imply that everything is now different. Rather, it is to argue that we need to carefully contextualise and understand the changes the war in Ukraine has amplified and accelerated. This needs to recognise the breaks with the past, even as we can see echoes of previous wars resonating across our social media feeds. This is important because the smartphone has become the technological enabler for collapsing the once distinct categories of soldier and civilian into the shared realm of participant. Everyone can engage in kinetic actions or influence activities, no matter where they are in the world.

In this respect, much of what is new on the battlefield reflects wider changes in society and its relationship to connected technology. These changes are not concerned simply with the online echo chambers that amplify identity politics but also with the technologies that now frame the ways in which people live and work in the digital realm. Big Tech, working with governments, have tried to algorithmically intervene to refashion discussion and debate. But the asymmetry in access between those who see everything and those who must rely on open-source information to understand war creates a knowledge gap. This is the gap that is being exploited for political purposes. War in Ukraine has precipitated cohesion in Ukrainian society. Conversely, Western citizens are struggling to sustain their interest or attention in the context of a fragmented media ecosystem and a cost-of-living crisis. In this context, the war in Ukraine may yet produce the shattering of resolve among Western nations who otherwise wish to hide from the dramatic geopolitical consequences of Russia's invasion.

1. The shutdown: conflict. *The Documentary Podcast*. BBC World Service, 16 March 2022, https:www.bbc.co.uk/programmes/p0bw07pw.

2. Stephen Fidler and Thomas Grove. Smartphones are changing the war in Ukraine. *Wall Street Journal*, 16 February 2023, https:www.wsj.com/articles/smartphones-are-changing-the-war-in-ukraine-adb37ba1.

3. Matthew Ford. From innovation to participation: the smartphone, connectivity and the conduct of contemporary warfare. *International Affairs*, Special Section, July 2024 (forthcoming).

4. Roman Horbyk. 'The war phone': mobile communication on the frontline in Eastern Ukraine. *Digital War*, vol 3, no 1, 2022, pp. 9–24.

5. Matthew Ford. Ukraine, participation and the smartphone at war. *Political Anthropological Research on International Social Sciences*, 2023, pp. 1–29.

6. Mike Moore. Ukraine hails 'priceless' help from Amazon Web Services. *Tech Radar*, 6 December 2022, https:www.techradar.com/news/ukraine-hails-priceless-help-from-amazon-web-services.

7. How a chatbot has turned Ukrainian civilians into digital resistance fighters. *The Economist*, 22 February 2023, https:www.economist.com/the-economist-explains/2023/02/22/how-a-chatbot-has-turned-ukrainian-civilians-into-digital-resistance-fighters.

8. A new era of transparent warfare beckons. *The Economist*, 18 February 2022, https:www.economist.com/briefing/2022/02/18/a-new-era-of-transparent-warfare-beckons.

9. Matthew Ford and Andrew Hoskins. *Radical War: Data, Attention and Control in the 21st Century*. New York: Oxford University Press, 2022.

10. Ukraine Digital Development Dashboard, ITU statistics. Dashboard available at https:www.itu.int/en/ITU-D/Statistics/Dashboards/Pages/Digital-Development.aspx.

11. Jack Hewson. A private company is using social media to track down Russian soldiers. *Foreign Policy*, 2 March 2023, https:foreignpolicy.com/2023/03/02/ukraine-russia-war-military-social-media-osint-open-source-intelligence/.

12. Frank Bajak. A chilling Russian cyber aim in Ukraine: digital dossiers. *AP News*, 28 April 2022, https:apnews.com/article/russia-ukraine-technology-business-border-patrols-automobiles-fa3f88e07e51bcaf81bac8a40c4da141.

13. Dunstan Allison-Hope. Our human rights impact assessment of Facebook in Myanmar, 5 November 2018, https:www.bsr.org/en/our-insights/blog-view/facebook-in-myanmar-human-rights-impact-assessment.

14. See Tim Judah speaking on *The Intelligence* podcast from *The Economist*, broadcast 5 April 2022. Relevant commentary from 3 minutes 30 seconds.

15. Jack Goodman and Maria Korenyuk. AI: war crimes evidence erased by social media platforms. BBC News, 1 June 2023, https:www.bbc.com/news/technology-65755517.

16. Kubo Mačák. Will the centre hold? Countering the erosion of the principle of distinction on the digital battlefield. *International Review of the Red Cross*, vol 105, no 923, 2023, pp. 965–91.
17. Justin Hendrix. Ukraine may mark a turning point in documenting war crimes. *Just Security*, 28 March 2022, https:www.justsecurity.org/80871/ukraine-may-mark-a-turning-point-in-documenting-war-crimes/.

CONTRIBUTORS

GILL BENNETT, Historian and former Chief Historian of the Foreign and Commonwealth Office.

SARA BUSH CASTRO, Associate Professor of History at the United States Air Force Academy, Colorado Springs, and President, Society for Intelligence History.

PHILIP HJ DAVIES, Professor of Intelligence Studies at Brunel University London and Director of the Brunel Centre for Intelligence and Security Studies.

JOHN FERRIS, emeritus Professor of History at the University of Calgary and Authorised Historian of the UK's Government Communications Headquarters.

MATTHEW FORD, Senior Lecturer and Associate Professor in the Department of War Studies at the Swedish Defence University.

MICHAEL GOODMAN, Professor of Intelligence and International Affairs and former Head of the Department of War Studies, Director of the King's Centre for the Study of Intelligence and Official Historian of the UK's Joint Intelligence Committee.

MATTHEW HEFLER, Postdoctoral Fellow at the Ax:son Johnson Institute for Statecraft and Diplomacy based at the Center for Statecraft and Strategic Communication, Stockholm School of Economics.

TONY INGESSON, Associate Senior Lecturer in the Department of Political Science at Lund University.

SUZANNE RAINE, Visiting Professor in the Department of War Studies, King's College London, and Deputy Chair of the Imperial War Museum.

DANIELA RICHTEROVA, Senior Lecturer in Intelligence Studies in the Department of War Studies, King's College London and Deputy Director of the King's Centre for the Study of Intelligence.

CALDER WALTON, Historian and Assistant Director of the Applied History Project and Intelligence Project at the Belfer Center for Science and International Affairs, John F. Kennedy School of Government, Harvard University.

STEVEN WAGNER, Senior Lecturer in International Security at Brunel University London.

Image rights ©

INTELLIGENCE AND CONTEMPORARY CONFLICT
Communication in Diplomacy, Statecraft and War

Published by Bokförlaget Stolpe, Stockholm, Sweden, 2024

© The authors and Bokförlaget Stolpe 2024

The essays are based on the seminar Intelligence, Communication and Contemporary Conflict
held at Engelsberg Ironworks in Västmanland, Sweden in 2023.

Edited by
Matthew Hefler, Research Fellow at the Center for Statecraft and Strategic Communication,
Stockholm School of Economics

Text editor: Andrew Mackenzie
Picture editor: Ann Lewenhaupt
Design: Patric Leo
Layout: Amelie Stenbeck Ramel and Pontus Dahlström
Cover image: Montfaucon, 1918. Osher Map Library and Smith Center for Cartographic Education
Prepress: Italgraf Media AB, Sweden
Print: Livonia Print, Latvia, 2024
First edition, first printing

ISBN: 978-91-89882-15-7

Bokförlaget Stolpe is a part of Axel and Margaret Ax:son Johnson Foundation for Public Benefit.

BOKFÖRLAGET STOLPE

AXEL AND MARGARET AX:SON JOHNSON
FOUNDATION FOR PUBLIC BENEFIT